Blue Plate Specials &
Blue Ribbon Chefs

Blue Plate

Blue

ALSO BY JANE AND MICHAEL STERN

*Square Meals • Eat Your Way Across the U.S.A. • Trucker: A Portrait of
the Last American Cowboy • Roadfood • Chili Nation • The Encyclopedia
of Bad Taste • Amazing America • Friendly Relations • Goodfood*

Specials & Ribbon Chefs

THE HEART AND SOUL OF AMERICA'S GREAT ROADSIDE-RESTAURANTS

Jane and Michael Stern

LEBHAR-FRIEDMAN BOOKS

NEW YORK · CHICAGO · LOS ANGELES · LONDON · PARIS · TOKYO

LEBHAR-FRIEDMAN BOOKS

A company of Lebhar-Friedman, Inc.

425 Park Avenue

New York, New York 10022

LIBRARY OF CONGRESS CATALOGING-IN-PUBLICATION DATA

Cataloging-in-publication data for this title is on file with the Library of Congress.

ISBN 0-86730-840-0

Designed and composed by Kevin Hanek

Set in FF Scala, FF Scala Sans, and Kaufmann

Manufactured in the United States of America on acid-free paper.

Visit our Web site at lfbooks.com

For John Porto –
trail boss, road-trip companion,
and good friend

Contents

Introduction

This is a book about celebrity chefs . . . although you may never have heard of any of them. Please believe us when we tell you that the men and women we wrote about are the talk of the town. The reason you might not know them is that the towns happen to be the likes of Tioga, Texas; or Social Circle, Georgia; or Havana, North Dakota.

Blue Plate Specials & Blue Ribbon Chefs is a collection of recipes and stories that reflect American food as we have come to know it while traveling several million miles in the last quarter century. It is an America of roadside diners, lunch counters, and neighborhood cafés, where the Dagwoodburgers and mile-high lemon pies are prepared with flair and passion unequalled by a five-hundred-dollar-a-plate dinner in New York's poshest restaurants.

This book will introduce you to people we consider America's true food heroes: short-order cooks, waitresses, barbecue pitmasters, bread bakers, pancake flippers, and maple-syrup mavens. We consider their stories and the recipes that go with them as something more than suggestions as to what to cook for dinner, because the kinds of restaurants we write about, in small towns or big cities, are much more than places to eat. They are the glue that holds a community together. Places like Snappy Lunch of Mount Airy, North Carolina, or Johnnie's Grill of El Reno, Oklahoma, are isles of human interaction in a sea of anonymous fast food.

At Manny's of Chicago, the city's top politicos dine shoulder to shoulder with the West Side's Foam Rubber King, and the salesclerk from the outlet store across the street that specializes in shoes up to size 16EEE. Regulars at the old neighborhood cafeteria know that Manny's serves the best potato pancakes and oxtail soup in Chicago but, just as important, they know each other. The people who put the food on your plate will likely remember if you like your pastrami fat or lean; the cashier knows whose husband just had a hip replacement; and good customers all know that you must go to Manny's early on Saint Patrick's Day, for the corned beef and cabbage in this Jewish delicatessen is devoured before the end of lunch hour by the Jews, Irish, African Americans, and members of the city's countless other ethnic groups, who all feel so at home at Manny's tables.

At Becky's, a diner on the waterfront in Portland, Maine, Becky Rand boasts a money-back guarantee: If you don't like your meal, you don't pay for it. Becky, a single mother of six who put all her children through school by working like a stevedore, is also Portland's culinary *über*mother. If a regular customer doesn't show up for breakfast or lunch, she will call the person at home or work to make sure everything's okay and, if it isn't, she will likely bring by a bowl of haddock chowder and a piece of layer cake to make things better.

In writing this book, we wanted to invite readers to join us at the Formica counters and café tables of places that we have loved over the years . . . and to meet the people we have met, and to eat the meals we will never forget. As we see it, dining out is a ritual of coming together, a way people express their heritage and sense of self. For us Americans, our myriad styles of eating are a truly awesome crazy quilt that defies easy definition. No doubt about it: This is a book of American food: food that is influenced by the cuisines of the world and cooks from nearly every nation. Here are Polish chop suey from Chicago, St. Paul sandwiches (egg foo yong on white bread with lettuce and tomato) from St. Louis, glorious Italian pastries from a tiny bakery in the roughhouse district of Pittsburgh known as the Strip, and liver 'n' onions from Al's Place in the Chinese community of Locke, California. America's menu is as diverse and as eccentric as our population.

Unlike French, Italian, or Japanese chefs, who build their skills on a venerable culinary history and learn to cook according to formal paradigms, America's cooks tend to feel unbounded by rules and snobbery. If it tastes good, we will eat it, and our restaurants are an ebullient reflection of that free spirit. We cannot imagine a better way to get to know the heart and soul of this country than by sitting down to eat at the everyday tables where blue plate specials are served.

Blue Plate Specials & Blue Ribbon Chefs is a book of recipes we like, and hope you will like, too. But we also want these pages to inspire you to disbelieve the myth that America has become one homogenized strip mall from sea to sea. *It has not.* To know this for certain, you only have to pull up a chair, stay a while, talk to the townsfolk, and listen to what they have to say. We guarantee you won't leave hungry . . . and that the overwhelming vastness of this huge country will seem very much like home.

The A-1 Diner

*T*he A-1 Diner, perched on steel stilts by the Cobbosseeconte Stream Bridge in an old mill town, is a radiant vision of short-order beauty. An enameled metal-and-mahogany Worcester dining car made to evoke sleek rolling stock in midcentury America, its decorative charms include the original tiny-octagon-tile floor, a worn-smooth marble counter, and scalloped stainless steel back wall. Some time after its installation in 1946, a kitchen was added to the rear, along with washrooms, which are accessible by walking out the front door and around the side on a creaky catwalk above the river bed.

At first glance, the menu appears to be a precise corollary to the setting, a roster of quintessential diner eats: franks 'n' beans, chicken pot pie, bowls of chili, fried tripe (a lunchtime tradition among diehard down-Easters), and tapioca pudding for dessert. But study the moveable-letter menu above the counter and you see gorgonzola risotto cakes, cardamom chicken stew, and chocolate hazelnut cake with hazelnut semi-freddo for dessert!

Fashionable food (and a wine list) in a vintage hash house is a happy incongruity created by Michael Giberson and Neil Anderson, who took over the old restaurant from Michael's father in 1988. "We didn't want to throw away the diner menu or the diner ambiance," Michael told us one lunch hour, in a wood-backed booth, over a plate of swoonfully creamy crab cakes dotted with kernels of corn. "And we couldn't afford to lose the local clientele. So, instead of making this place into something it was not, we have tried to make it into the best possible diner. After all, that is why we are here—we like diners!"

The first thing Michael and Neil did when they took over was to eliminate all frozen and packaged products, replacing soggy biscuits with flaky, from-scratch ones expertly made by Robert Newell, who has been an A-1 cook since the 1950s. They knew they had a master of diner-style cookery in Bob, so they assigned him to prepare the mashed potatoes; it is he who is in charge of corned-beef hash, a frequent dinner special. Gradually, they started adding more exotic dishes to the menu in hopes of attracting a culinarily adventurous crowd in addition to—but not in place of—the meat-and-potatoes regulars.

Cindy, the waitress (for thirty-five years now), appears a little more comfortable taking orders for and serving beef stew or grilled knockwurst with onions but, each day, her order pad is augmented by a crib sheet that allows her to scrupulously enumerate the full list of ingredients for such wild and wonderful meals as fiddlehead-fern lasagna, Tuscan black-backed sole with Oriental greens, Vietnamese bouillabaisse, and eggplant pasticcio.

We have heard eaters at the counter moan with joy when spooning into the A-1's potato-celeriac-parsnip soup. A strange summertime lobster roll, with a Tex-Mex pepper twist, is an ecstatic surprise even for the most lobster-jaded palate. But, as culinary classicists, what sends us into orbit at the A-1 are its uncomplicated versions of what used to be diner standards throughout New England: honest omelets every morning, a repertoire of at least a half-dozen kinds of meatloaf, slow-cooked baked beans that are lusciously tasty (pork-free for vegetarians!), and such alluring desserts as red devil's food cake, Maine whoopie pie, and quivery, old-time, Grape-Nuts pudding.

"I hate that word *eclectic*," Michael says. "It is so overused. But I don't have a better one to describe what we do. For us, what's fun about this place is that we don't have to cook the same thing every day. If we find a recipe for wild rice-stuffed squash or kisela-juba soup or even ooey-gooey cake, we have no qualms about making some to see how people like it. Of course, there are everyday customers who would mutiny if we didn't have Bob's pancakes for breakfast and warm gingerbread with lemon sauce for dessert at lunch. This business still depends on locals coming in for simple meals—they are the lifeblood of any diner—but we also have customers who travel from Augusta or Portland, and beyond. You know, if you live in Maine and are a foodaholic, you must be willing to drive a long way for a good meal."

Gingerbread with Lemon Sauce

1 cup butter, softened

1 cup brown sugar

$^{1}/_{2}$ cup molasses

$^{1}/_{2}$ cup corn syrup

2 eggs, beaten

$^{1}/_{2}$ teaspoon salt

$2^{1}/_{2}$ cups all-purpose flour

2 teaspoons baking soda

1 cup buttermilk, at room temperature

8 ounces fresh ginger, minced

1 tablespoon powdered ginger

1. Preheat oven to 325°F. Butter a 9-by-13-inch baking pan.

2. Cream together butter and sugar. Add molasses, corn syrup, eggs, and salt. Beat until smooth.

3. Mix flour and baking soda. Whisk half the flour into the butter-sugar mixture, then add half the buttermilk. Repeat. Stir in gingers. Pour into prepared pan and bake, 40–45 minutes, or until center is puffed and cake tester or sharp knife comes out clean.

Lemon Sauce

Grated zest of 3 lemons

1 cup fresh lemon juice

$1^{1}/_{2}$ cups sugar

$^{1}/_{2}$ teaspoon salt

6 whole eggs

12 egg yolks

1 cup butter

1. Place zest, juice, sugar, salt, eggs, and yolks in stainless steel bowl over simmering water. Keep the water at a low simmer—do not boil!—and whisk mixture continuously until thick. Remove from heat and whisk in butter, tablespoon by tablespoon.

2. Serve warm, atop warm gingerbread.

Makes 6–8 servings.

Al's #1 Italian Beef

CHICAGO, ILLINOIS

*B*efore you eat a hot beef sandwich in Chicago, you need to talk to Chris Pacelli, Jr., who owns Al's with his brothers Chuck and Terry. He'll tell you how to do it right.

"Assume the stance," he honks in pure Chicago style, positioning himself at a chest-high ledge on which customers in his restaurant dine. "Put your feet apart and slide 'em back like you are going to be frisked. Put your two elbows on the counter and put both your hands on the sandwich, thumbs underneath." When he stands in this position, with his mitts enveloping a Big Al's beef sandwich—a shaft of fresh-baked bread loaded with warm sliced meat, garnished with sweet roasted peppers and hot giardiniera relish, and soaked with natural gravy—he looks like a giddy strangler with his fingers wrapped around a neck. "Now, bring it to your face." He pauses a delicious moment, when the sandwich is close enough, to smell its warm, beefy bouquet. His elbows never leave the counter as he opens wide to yank off a juicy chaw, then pulls what's left away to a nice viewing distance, relishing the sight of it, and the savor in his mouth. "See how all the juice drips on the counter, not on your shoes or shirt! That's because of the stance!"

In Chicago, where everybody knows this particular type of roast-beef sandwich as "Italian beef," the stance is as much a part of culinary culture as deep-dish pan pizza and Marshall Field's Frango mints. Thin-sliced beef sopped in gravy and stuffed into the absorbent maw of a fresh loaf from Gonnella bakery is the city's premier street food.

Inside the little cement-floored shed that is Al's, every available eating surface is elbow to elbow with beef aficionados, their hands glistening with juice, their eyes on their sandwiches. The far end of the order counter has room for about ten stand-up eaters, where the scenery is a vista of sausages sputtering over charcoal. Two sides of the rectangular shop offer gleaming silver counters and picture windows with views of the parking lot and the sidewalk. The din is deafening: customers calling out orders and the staff behind the counter calling back at them. The dialogue is eloquent eat-shop shorthand.

"Big beef, double-dipped!" is an extra-large sandwich of gravy-sopped beef that, once assembled, is reimmersed very quickly in a pan of natural gravy, so the bread is soaked through.

"Beef with hot" is a request for the relish known as *giardiniera,* an eye-opening garden mélange of finely chopped marinated vegetables, capers, and spices that is roast beef's perfect complement. The Pacelli brothers make their giardiniera in thirty-gallon batches, and let it ferment three to four days until it's ready.

"Dry and sweet!" tells the sandwich maker to pluck a heap of beef from its pan with the serving tongs and let excess juice drip away before inserting it in the bread.

"Sweet" is the popular alternative to giardiniera: big, tender shreds of roasted green bell pepper. Some customers order double hot or double sweet; some get their sandwich sweet *and* hot.

"Combo!" or "half and half!" is a call for a sandwich that contains not only beef but also a plump, four-inch length of Italian sausage, retrieved from the appetizing haze that hovers over the hot metal grate just behind the order counter. "Our charcoal is grandfathered in," Chris Pacelli boasts, explaining that Chicago law requires any new Italian beef stand to cook its sausage on a gas grill. Coals give Al's taut-skinned tubes of peppery, coarse-ground pork a sharp, smoky flavor. Succulent and well spiced, the sausage is itself a major lure for many customers who sidestep beef altogether and order double-sausage sandwiches, hot or sweet, dipped or dry.

But the main reason for Al's legendary status in Chicago is beef, which the Pacellis create by putting three twelve-pound sirloin butts in the oven at a time, layering them in a silver pot full of spices, including several whole bulbs of garlic that Chris has crushed between his palms. When they have cooked at least three hours, they are retrieved from their spicy cooking juices, which are poured through a superfine strainer, yielding an unclouded, mahogany broth. The broth is diluted and simmered atop the stove, gradually becoming the precious dipping juice in which beef is immersed just before serving, and into which some whole sandwiches are plunged. After the slabs of beef have cooled and settled overnight, all their fat is cut away and they are sliced extremely thin. Without the additional immersion in the juice, these slices are dry, albeit high flavored and butter tender. At this point in the preparation, a condition of supreme purity has been attained. On the cutting board is a pile of impeccable lean beef and on the stove is a pot of clear beef essence. Now, the trick is to combine the two. Years of practice have taught the Pacellis precisely when to dunk beef in the pan of hot juices, so that it sops up maximum amounts of the savory liquid just before it gets piled into a sandwich.

Al's sells beef by the pound, and there are people who actually buy it to take home and serve on a plate, with knife and fork, like it was meat cut from an ordinary roast. Such amenities are anathema to most Chicagoans, for whom Italian beef means just one thing: a paper-wrapped sandwich at a curbside stand where they can assume the stance and savor a perfect harmony of meat and gravy, bakery-fresh bread, and the company of fellow connoisseurs.

Giardiniera for Beef Sandwiches

Traditional giardiniera recipes suggest breaking broccoli and cauliflower into bite-sized pieces, along with large slices of carrot and bell pepper. That's fine for a colorful side dish to be served on a plate but, for topping a beef sandwich, you need a relish so finely chopped that it spreads nicely with a spoon. Al's formula is not written down, but Chris Pacelli opened up the thirty-gallon tub in which a batch of giardiniera was fermenting, stirred it with a long wooden spoon, and gave us a few expert tips. He especially warned against using too much garlic or too much red pepper, thereby creating a condiment that calls attention to itself. A good giardiniera should have just enough zest to underscore—but not overwhelm—the deep, mellow savor of the juicy beef.

3 celery ribs, minced

1 small clove garlic, minced

1/2 red pepper, seeded and minced

1 plum tomato, finely chopped

2 tablespoons small capers with 1 tablespoon caper juice

1/2 teaspoon dried, crushed red-pepper flakes

1 teaspoon dried oregano

1/3 cup olive oil

2 tablespoons lemon juice

Combine all ingredients, toss to mix, and cover. Let the mixture steep, refrigerated, at least 24 hours, preferably 48, tossing a few times each day. Keeps about a week, chilled.

Makes enough to generously top 6 sandwiches.

Al's Diner

*T*o learn about Al's Diner of Minneapolis, we requested an audience with Philip Bergstrom, nephew of counterculture patron saint Al Bergstrom. Philip arrived for our meeting at the diner one morning dressed in jeans, work shirt, and porkpie hat, with a stylish two-day beard, sort of like a Bruce Willis manqué. "I'll tell you the whole story of this place," he said, swirling coffee in his cup with glee, "but I'm warning you, it's all lies."

In the 1930s, what is now Al's was an alleyway between two stores in the University of Minnesota neighborhood called Dinkytown. The proprietor of one of the stores covered a short length of the alley so it could be used as a machine shop in all weather. In 1938, the covered space was transformed into a diner called Hunky Dory Lunch. Some time in the early 1940s, a fellow named Bill bought Hunky Dory and renamed it Bill's Place. Dinkytown was thick with tenement housing for war-effort workers and there were nearly two-dozen blue-collar lunchrooms in the area to feed them. Bill started selling books of meal tickets so that patrons wouldn't drink up all their paychecks.

As Philip stands in the kitchen, drinking coffee and regaling us with tales of his Uncle Al's days as a bootleg yeast distributor during Prohibition, John Marshall walks through the back door and joins the history lesson. Friends of Al's frequently come in through the back door to have a quick cup of coffee on their way to work or school. John, an artist and set designer, fetches his own cup and makes himself comfortable leaning against the syrup and salsa shelf in the kitchen, adding his own reminiscences to Philip's chronicle.

In 1950, Al Bergstrom bought Bill's Place. "He and the family and a friend combined their savings and paid a grand total of six hundred dollars for the business," Philip says.

John Marshall chimes in with a sly grin: "It's got to be worth at least a thousand now!"

Al's started as a three-meal-a-day restaurant, with a bank of ovens stationed in the back kitchen. However, around 1960, Al's doctor said he'd better slow down. He took a poll among customers, asking which meal they liked best, and it was decided that Al would limit himself to breakfast.

Philip started working for his uncle as a dishwasher in 1970; in 1973 he bought the business. "I tried to buy the building, too," he recalls, "but I found that I couldn't because it is not a building. It is an alley with a roof."

Small is not a little enough word to describe what Al's is. Measuring a diminutive ten by eight feet—actually 790 square feet altogether—it is built around an ancient counter of worn yellow linoleum, with twelve stools permanently attached in an aisle in which any good-sized person has to walk sideways to pass between them and the wall behind. At each end of the counter, there is one extra portable stool, raising the total seating capacity to fourteen. The kitchen area stretches the length of the counter and into a sort of bay area at the front window where the cook works a grill, flipping pancakes and corned-beef hash, and tending a waffle iron. Near the grill is a stove with two boiling pots for poaching eggs. There are five

people altogether behind the counter at any one time, but it seems like many more. The cook in back breezes up front to deliver trays of raw eggs to the grill man; the grill man floats back to pick up vinegar for his poaching water. A couple of waitresses patrol the counter, armed with coffee pots for refills.

There is always plenty of noise behind the counter:

"Two with cheddar and sausage, butter, and a short stack," a waitress calls toward the front. A short stack is two pancakes. A short-short is one. A long stack is four.

"Scramble two on an oval!" the grill man hollers into the back kitchen, referring to an oval plate, which means that he needs room for a heap of hash browns.

"Two with smoky on a round," a waitress yells into the back. Smoky means smoky cheddar cheese, which is scrambled with the eggs, and—unless you say differently—with plenty of cream and butter. The round plate has no room for potatoes.

"Benny, double holly!" is the call for eggs Benedict with extra hollandaise.

A steady customer joins the fun, sitting on a stool and bellowing, "Dogfood and two pooched." He gets corned-beef hash with two poached eggs on top.

"Here's a Norwegian hors d'oeuvre while you wait," says Doug Grina, the day's chef, as he walks along behind the counter carrying a dime-sized pancake on his spatula—a mere drip from the griddle. He flips the miniature pancake onto a plate and pushes it across the counter toward a seated customer.

"You're late!" Doug barks at a pair of old friends who arrive for breakfast at 6:45 instead of their usual 6:15.

Doug has a hard time getting an over-easy egg order just right. "I cooked this guy's breakfast twice!" he announces to the fourteen people seated at the counter. "I hope you all know that I have no idea what I'm doing. I just put things in the toaster at random, and I'm not sure why."

Rose Jensen, a long-time waitress who wears a "Coffee Is God" lapel pin, picks up the ill-starred fried-egg order, which Doug has finally gotten right, gives it a once-over on its way to the counter, and says in a stage mutter for all to hear, "Now I know what not to have for breakfast."

"What are you trying to do, get healthy?" Doug razzes a student who has ordered her short stack dry, that is without a blob of butter melting on top.

"Here it comes," Rose announces as she totes a tub of butter up front for Doug to use. "Here's the favorite dish we serve at Al's." (Butter is a regional obsession not unique to Al's. It is at least as big in Minnesota as in Wisconsin; at the annual State Fair, it is used to sculpt likenesses of all the Fair Queens.)

Breakfast at Al's seems like chaos, but it works. Nearly everybody gets what they order, even if they want their poached eggs rock hard or hash blackened or eggs over ultra-easy. It is *not* fast food, not like a franchise, anyway. Breakfast can take as long as twelve or fifteen minutes. Hash browns alone spend seven or eight minutes on the grill, more if you like them with a brittle surface. Because egg-poaching facilities are limited and poached eggs are popular, there is sometimes a backlog of orders. Nobody gripes about the wait, because few people come to Al's for a hurried, anonymous meal. Customers cherish time spent here. Each person at the counter becomes part of a ritual morning comedy that is at once unpredictable, yet reassuringly familiar.

A few years ago, in the doldrums of January, waitress Rose Jensen did her part to liven things up by inventing Hat and Jewelry Day, along with Mary Rose, another waitress. The first Thursday of every month, each borrows her daughters' tackiest jewelry and wears outrageous hats to work. However, Doug Grina outdid them both, showing up in full makeup, wearing a spangled dress and high-peaked princess hat. ("My in-laws love me like that!" he says with a goofy grin.) It was shortly after the inauguration of Hat and Jewelry Day, Rose recalls, that she found the man of her dreams—at the counter of Al's, where else? She was in the kitchen and he came in with a buddy. He and his friend traded wisecracks with the help and, as Rose and he listened to each other talk, they fell in love. He is a neon artist who is also a hot-mustard fanatic. Al's has plenty of Tabasco sauce and ketchup, but no mustard, so Rose's guy brought his own. "He takes mustard everywhere he goes," she says with a happy blush. "He puts it on everything, even his oatmeal."

Kibitzer extraordinnaire John Marshall, who has never officially worked at Al's, but who brags that he had earned "free short-stack privileges until the year 2000" in exchange for some shelves he built to hold the coffee cups, listened to Rose's story, nodding his head in agreement. She has proven a favorite point of his: That magic things happen in this old diner. "It is an organism," he explains. "It is not some soulless concept restaurant that a corporate idea man at a drawing board designed. Good things happen here; people's lives change. If you want a car, or an apartment, or a sweetheart, come in and sit at the counter. Come in, have coffee, and chat a while. Pretty soon, I promise, you will get what you need. Al's has a life of its own, above and beyond any of us. I truly believe it is a crossroads of the universe."

Al's Buttermilk Pancakes

DRY MIX
- 3 cups white flour
- 1 teaspoon salt
- 1½ teaspoons sugar
- 2½ teaspoons baking powder
- ¾ teaspoon baking soda

WET MIX
- 4 cups buttermilk
- 2 extra large eggs, beaten
- 3 tablespoons melted butter

OPTIONAL
- 1 pint blueberries, washed and dried
- *or* 1 pint blackberries, washed and dried
- *or* 1 cup chopped walnuts
- *or* 1 cup whole kernel corn

Butter, for the griddle

1. Separately combine dry and wet ingredients in two bowls. Combine the two mixtures, and let sit a while—at least 15 minutes, but even overnight (refrigerated) is fine. If the batter sits overnight, stir it well before pouring; you may need to thin it with a bit more buttermilk.

2. Blueberries or blackberries may be mixed into the batter if desired.

3. Heat a griddle or large cast-iron skillet to medium heat. Melt butter on the griddle. Pour out 6-inch diameter pancakes. Sprinkle with walnuts or corn, if desired. When most of the bubbles on top of the cake begin to pop, flip the pancake, and cook it about a minute more. Serve immediately.

Makes 10–12 large pancakes; serving 4–6.

Al's Place

*7*he levee town of Locke, in the Sacramento Delta, was built in 1912 by and for Chungshan Chinese, and used to be known for its gambling halls, houses of ill repute, and last—maybe least—of its pleasures, Cantonese food. Locke is ghostly today, with less than one-hundred residents left; and its weathered main street of raised side-walks and shuttered emporia with swayback second-story balconies remains a magical sight. In the middle of all this is Al's Place, thriving since 1934, when Al Adami, fresh out of prison for bootlegging, opened up the only non-Chinese restaurant in town. Al had no menu—he asked you how you liked your steak, which was the only thing to eat amidst the slot machines and card tables in the dining room behind the front-room bar. Legend says that, at some point, a hungry cropduster came in with jars of peanut butter and marmalade and asked Al for some toast to spread them on. Al liked the idea, and started putting peanut butter and marmalade on every table, a strange tradition that has endured to this day.

Now run by Stephen and Lorenzo Giannetti, Al's Place still feels illicit. You enter past the beer-and-shooter crowd, who occupy a dimly lit bar hung with dusty game trophies and memorabilia, into a bright back-room dining area lined with worn laminate tables equipped with shared benches (instead of chairs), seating anywhere from two to eight friends or strangers, depending on how crowded Al's is. The old wood floor creaks as Stephen Giannetti carries steaks to the tables and, in lieu of music, the room is serenaded by a constant sizzle of meat from the adjoining kitchen.

The menu remains simple, now including hamburgers, cheese-burgers, and steak sandwiches, in addition to steak. The burgers are juicy ones, served between thick slices of grilled, crisp Italian bread with lettuce, tomato, onions, pickle, and olives on the side. The steak sandwich is, in fact, not a sandwich, but a sandwich-sized steak on a platter, accompanied by a second plate of toasted pieces of sturdy Italian bread. Horseradish or a dish of minced garlic are available to spread on the

meat. "Most people put the peanut butter or marmalade on their toast," Stephen advises us when we ask him what to do with it. "But I've seen some spread peanut butter right across their steaks!"

When we ask him if he hears any complaints about the name by which regular customers know the restaurant, and which is emblazoned on its front door—Al the Wop's—he answers flatly, "No," as if only some sort of dimwit pedant would worry about such a politically correct nonissue. He then continues: "I am Italian, and I don't mind the word *wop*. It's all in how it is said, anyway. W.O.P. simply means without papers, the way so many Italians came to the U.S. as immigrants. What's wrong with that?"

From a nearby table, a compatriot eating a steak sandwich adds to the conversation by asking, "Do you know why so many of us Italians are called Tony?" When we shrug uncomfortably at this line of discourse, he answers himself by explaining that a lot of immigrants on Ellis Island who could not speak English got a ticket that read "To N.Y." He and the boss laugh so hard that they look like they might tumble onto the floor.

On the way out, through the barroom in front, we happen to notice that the high ceiling, far out of reach for even the tallest person, is crowded with dollar bills affixed with thumbtacks. Mickey the bartender tells us that money on the ceiling is a tradition that goes back to Al's era, but it will cost a dollar to find out how it gets there. Okay, we're game. We give Mickey a folding bill, which he somehow curls around a thumbtack and a heavy silver dollar. In the blink of an eye, he flips this package upward. All that comes down is his silver dollar. Apparently, the dollar that used to be ours is now tacked to Al's ceiling.

"What happens when the ceiling is full of money?" we ask.

"It is harvested in the winter," Mickey answers, "It goes toward the big February liver feed. We cook liver 'n' onions for the whole town—free."

Liver 'n' Onions

Steaks or burgers are what we recommend eating if you visit Al's Place but, like the citizens of Locke, we have a special fondness for liver and onions—a dish we, too, prepare about once a year in mass quantities for ourselves. This is our favorite way to make it. Of course, bacon is optional. If you want bacon, cook it first in the skillet, remove it and pour off the excess grease, using the residue to cook the onions. If no bacon grease is available, use a half-and-half combination of butter and oil. Calf's liver is very delicate and gets tough if cooked much beyond rare. Beef liver can be coarse but holds up to the heat better. The cut we recommend is what's known as baby beef liver, which is not quite as rugged, but has more character than calf's liver.

3 tablespoons butter	1 pound liver, sliced about $1/4$-inch thick, membrane removed before slicing.
3 tablespoons oil	
$1\frac{1}{2}$ cups thinly sliced onion	

1. Combine butter and oil in a heavy skillet over medium heat. Add onion and stir, almost constantly, until the onion is all soft, and almost as brown as you like your onions.

2. Scoot onions to edge of pan and raise heat to high. (You may find it necessary—or desirable—to add a few more tablespoons of oil and butter, especially if the pan is not well seasoned, and if you like more luscious liver.) Slap slices of liver into the pan and cook 1 minute, no more. Flip and cook, up to 1 minute more, depending on how well done you want them. As liver cooks, scoot onion around and on top of it. Serve liver heaped with sautéed onions and sided by real mashed potatoes.

Makes 4 servings.

Anchor Inn

FARRAGUT, IOWA

lthough unnoted by the bicoastal food establishment, one of the great culinary events of 1999 was the reopening of the Anchor Inn of Farragut, Iowa. The small-town café in the state's south-western farmland had been a beacon of good eats—of great cinnamon buns, in particular—throughout most of the 1980s, when it was run by Emmy Bengston. When it closed in 1993, Iowans, and devotees of Iowa café cooking mourned. The proprietors for the new millennium, Rhonda and Steve McDonald, are the daughter-in-law and son of Mrs. Bengsten and, when they reopened her place (all remodeled and spanking clean), they coaxed Emmy out of retirement to make cinnamon buns.

When we tell you that Emmy's buns are big—hot, yeasty swirls veined with cinnamon sugar and dripping white-sugar glaze—please try to imagine them, then quadruple the size you have imagined. These buns are giants, approximately six inches square and four inches high, and they are delectable. Back during her original tenure, Mrs. Bengston told us her secret: "Potato water with all those nice potato goodies from the bottom of the pot." Potato water—water in which you have boiled potatoes—rather than ordinary warm water, gives Emmy's buns a softness and flavor that make them, in our cinnamon-bun-eating experience, the best in Iowa—a state where cinnamon buns reign as the supreme bakery treat.

Emmy always has plenty of potato water available, because the Anchor Inn always serves freshly mashed potatoes for lunch. Most plate lunches come with billowy spuds, often smothered with good brown gravy. Potatoheads like ourselves could make a meal of them. And, oh, what a chicken fried steak comes alongside these potatoes! It is crisp-crusted, tender enough inside to be a pleasant chew, but with real beef flavor that overly tenderized meat never has. Also on the daily menu are such heartland dishes as Polish sausage and sauerkraut, meatloaf, ham loaf, and chicken 'n' biscuits. Alongside come vegetables—vegetables from a garden, cooked and bathed in butter. Even the simple buttered

carrots we ate with our roast-beef dinner remain in our memory as some of the tastiest ever.

We're thrilled that, after several years without it, we can once again put the Anchor Inn in our little black book of four-star farmland cafés. It remains what it has always been: the heart of its community and a treasure for any traveler in search of Iowa on a plate. Evelyn Birkby, the grande dame of Shenandoah, Iowa's radio homemakers (who has broadcast cooking tips on station KMA since the early days of radio in the 1920s) was the person who originally took us there, then shared this precious recipe, courtesy of Emmy.

Emmy's Big Buns

- 1 package yeast
- 2 tablespoons warm water (105–110°F)
- 4 tablespoons (¹/₂ stick), plus 2 table-spoons margarine, melted
- 1¹/₂ cups warm potato water (105–110°F), or substitute ¹/₄ cup dry instant mashed potatoes and 1¹/₂ cups water
- 1/3 cup sugar
- 1 teaspoon salt

- ¹/₂ cup nonfat dry milk
- 2 eggs, lightly beaten
- 4–5 cups all-purpose flour
- 1 cup sugar
- ¹/₄ cup brown sugar
- 1 tablespoon ground cinnamon
- 2 tablespoons butter, softened
- 1 tablespoon water
- 1¹/₂ cups confectioners' sugar

1. Dissolve yeast in 2 tablespoons of warm water. When yeast is foamy, mix it with 4 tablespoons margarine, potato water (or plain water and dry instant potatoes), sugar, salt, nonfat dry milk, eggs, and 4 cups flour. Mix until a ragged dough begins to form, adding flour as needed.

2. Turn dough out on floured board and knead, 5 minutes, adding flour as needed, to make a smooth, silky dough. Roll dough into ball and place in a greased bowl, cover and let rise in a warm, place 1–2 hours, until doubled in bulk.

3. Grease a baking pan, about 10-by-10 inches, or an ovenproof 12-inch skillet.

4. Turn dough out on floured board, knead, 1 minute, and roll into a rectangle about $1/2$-inch high. Brush with remaining 2 tablespoons melted margarine. Combine sugars and cinnamon and sprinkle onto buttered dough. Roll dough up like a jellyroll, and cut into 6 slices. Place the slices in the prepared baking pan, cut side up, cover loosely and let rise until nearly doubled, about 45 minutes.

5. Preheat oven to 375°F. Bake risen rolls 35–40 minutes.

6. As rolls bake, make glaze by beating butter and water into confectioners' sugar (you may need up to $1^1/2$ tablespoons of water to make a thick, spoonable glaze).

7. When rolls are still warm from the oven, spoon on glaze.

Makes 6 big buns.

Becky's

ecky Rand was a woman on a mission when she opened Becky's at the wharf in Portland in 1991. "Workers from the boats and the docks had nowhere to eat!" she says with sincere astonishment. Back then, a few upscale dining rooms had opened in the historic cobblestone-street district, which, although still perfumed by the fishing fleet, has since become a stylish place to shop and dine. However, those restaurants charged double-digit prices and didn't want a blue-collar crowd. "Men in work clothes scared off their customers," Becky says. "I asked myself, 'Where is the nice, hot meal for the all-night cab drivers, the scallop draggers and lobstermen getting an early start, cops on the beat, and the luckless guy or gal scraping together dimes and quarters to buy a grilled-cheese sandwich and a cup of coffee?'"

Living lean was something Becky Rand knew all about. Then in her mid-thirties, she had been left with six children to support, which she tried to do by simultaneously working three different waitressing jobs and by baking for local restaurants. "I went to five different banks pleading for money to open my own place, and they couldn't show me the door fast enough," she remembers. With little more than steadfast determination as collateral, she finally convinced one bank officer to loan her money to start a short-order café in a boarded-up building by the water at Hobson's Wharf. With secondhand equipment in the kitchen and decrepit booths salvaged from a restaurant-supply warehouse, Becky's opened with a staff of two. "That first day, I did all the cooking and washed so many dishes, my hands bled," she recalls. "I hadn't hired a dishwasher because I didn't think I'd need one."

Successful from the beginning, Becky's is now mobbed every morning, starting at four, and is open every day of the year except Thanksgiving and Christmas. Becky loves the variety of her clientele. "No matter who you are out there, when you walk into Becky's Diner, you are one of us," she says. "We have people come in here who are scraping together their last dollar for a grilled-cheese sandwich and a cup of coffee, and we have the biggest lawyers in town. Side by side at my counter sit fishermen and captains of industry, college professors and paranoid schizophrenics. They talk to each other and they talk to those who work here. We are all family."

Becky's family reference isn't just figurative. She means it *literally*; each of her children has worked in the diner: Her oldest daughter recently put herself through college on tips; her sister is a behind-the-counter regular; her parents have lunch in a booth every day; and her dad mops the floor each afternoon.

The bustling dining room is big and comfortable, with a few tables up front, upholstered booths along one wall, and a long counter lined with chrome-banded stools, which face the kitchen window, where orders are hung on clothespins. The view of the counter just below the kitchen window is an appetizing one: muffins getting buttered, coffee beans being ground, and plated meals still sizzling and smoking on their way to customers. Coffee is poured in thick china mugs, and served with a spoon already planted in the brew, ready to stir; even when every seat in the house is occupied, you can count on the omniscient waitresses to top off your cup at approximately every other sip.

All meals at Becky's are backed by a no-strings-attached *one-hundred percent guarantee*: If you don't like it, you don't pay. ("I stole that from L. L. Bean," Becky says with home-state pride in Freeport's conspicuously prosperous outfitter.) Using her own hand-me-down recipes as well as those she finds in vintage cookbooks, Becky offers daily specials of such sure-to-please diner paragons as meatloaf with mashed potatoes, roast turkey with sausage stuffing, slow-baked beans with franks, and—every Friday—haddock chowder. "We always have the freshest haddock," Becky boasts, "usually from just down the street." Like an of-the-people Alice Waters, she gets much of her fish, as well as the good breads and summer fruits and vegetables, from local sources.

"We have many customers who eat here every day, some twice, for breakfast *and* for supper," Becky says. A while ago, there was one such Mr. Predictable who didn't come in for his usual meal one morning.

Becky and the waitresses got to talking about him and, by late in the day, when he didn't show up yet again, they were worried. So they looked him up in the phone book and called to find out why he was suddenly so scarce. Sure enough, he was home with a cold. So, of course, one of the staff brought him a container of warm soup. Becky tells of another couple—mentally challenged sweethearts who live in a group home nearby—who are thoughtful enough to telephone the diner on those days when they are *not* coming in for lunch!

Every-Friday Haddock Chowder

Customers from all over Portland know Friday as chowder day at Becky's. The dish is a luxurious meal unto itself.

6 tablespoons margarine

1 cup chopped onion

1 teaspoon black pepper

1 teaspoon garlic powder

$1/2$ teaspoon salt

6 cups diced raw potato (peeled)

2 pounds skinless haddock fillets (a little over 2 pounds)

4 cans evaporated whole milk

2 cups whole milk

6 strips bacon, cooked crisp, and broken into pieces

1. In a deep saucepan or Dutch oven, melt the margarine. Add the onion and sauté until transparent. Add pepper, garlic powder, salt, and potatoes, plus enough water to barely cover the potatoes. Boil until potatoes are tender, about 10 minutes.

2. Lay the haddock atop cooked potatoes and onions. Do not drain off water or add more. Cover the pan and boil over medium heat until the fish flakes apart with a fork, about 8 minutes.

3. Add evaporated milk and whole milk and heat, but do not return to boil.

4. Add bacon, and additional salt and pepper, to taste.

Makes 8–10 servings.

Becky's Whoopie-Pie Cake with Poor-Man's Icing

The whoopie pie was invented in Maine back in the 1920s: Like a giant, squishy Oreo cookie, it is two discs of chocolate cake sandwiching a creamy-sweet filling. One of Becky's most popular desserts is a cake she makes inspired by the whoopie pie, frosted with a low-cost icing she found while browsing through a World War II era cookbook. The marshmallow-soft icing gives this cake an evocative old-fashioned character, totally unlike a modern "sinful" boutique gâteau.

1 cup margarine

2 cups sugar

2$\frac{1}{4}$ cups all-purpose flour

1 teaspoon baking soda

1 teaspoon salt

1$\frac{1}{4}$ cups buttermilk

3 eggs

9 tablespoons cocoa powder

ICING

2 cups whole milk

$\frac{3}{4}$ cup all-purpose flour

2 cups sugar

8 tablespoons butter

1 tablespoon vanilla

1 cup solid vegetable shortening

1. Preheat oven to 350°F. Grease two 9-inch round cake pans.

2. Beat together the margarine and sugar. Add flour, baking soda, and salt. Mix slowly, gradually adding buttermilk. Beat, 2 full minutes. Add eggs, then gradually add cocoa, beating another 2 minutes, stopping occasionally to scrape the sides of the bowl.

3. Pour batter into prepared pans and bake, about 40 minutes, until center springs back when gently pushed.

4. Cool, 5 minutes, then remove cakes from pans and cool completely on a wire rack.

5. To make the icing, pour the milk into a saucepan over medium heat. Gradually whisk in flour until a thick paste forms. Do not scorch! Remove from stove and cool this mixture in the refrigerator.

6. In a separate bowl, mix the sugar, butter, vanilla, and shortening. Add the cooled paste. Whip, at least 3 minutes, until creamy.

Makes enough icing to generously frost a 2-layer cake.

Blue Willow Inn

SOCIAL CIRCLE, GEORGIA

"We knew one thing when we opened," explained Louis Van Dyke, proprietor of the Blue Willow Inn, as we joined him in a round of what he referred to as "the champagne of the South"—presweetened iced tea. "We were going to have to serve meals that people would be willing to drive an hour to eat. We would have to be that good, or the Blue Willow Inn didn't have a chance."

The Blue Willow Inn *is* that good. Atlantans think nothing of driving an hour to eat at the grand Greek Revival mansion in the village of Social Circle. Augustans drive two hours and, on weekends, families travel from Tennessee and the Carolinas to make a day of the sumptuous event. "We have two rules here," the waitress warns us at the beginning of a meal, after asking if we prefer our tea sweetened or unsweetened, then pointing us toward the buffet. "Rule one is that no one goes home hungry. Rule two is that everybody has to have at least two desserts."

The heart of the inn is the buffet room, where customers help themselves. Here you find a salad table, a soup table, a lengthy U-shaped table with pans of hot meats and sizzling vegetables, and a large dessert table in the center of it all. It is a ravishing sight, but we caution you now: No matter how big an appetite you are packing when you arrive, it is absolutely impossible to have a satisfying serving of everything that tempts you. With a minimum of four different meats, and more than a dozen vegetables on display, not to mention the chicken 'n' dumpling soup and the biscuits and cornbread and relishes and puddings and salads and umpteen pies, cakes, cookies, brownies, and cobbler, you can either aim for a tiny bite of everything you like or make hard choices: pass up the opulent macaroni and cheese in favor of a nice-sized portion of skillet squash; ignore the cornbread dressing, so you have room on the plate for sweet corn casserole. If you crave a feast of baked and smothered pork chops, then you likely won't have a chance to appreciate the kitchen's magnificent streak o' lean—thick strips of bacony pork that vary in texture from wickedly crusty to meltaway lush, blanketed with smooth, white gravy. For those of us who travel far to eat at the Blue Willow Inn and can come only rarely, these decisions can be agonizing. Customers are welcome to return to the buffet for second, third, fourth, and fifth helpings, but some dishes are so darn delicious that you want to pile your plate with them again and again, recklessly sacrificing variety for monomaniacal satisfaction.

Certain basic foods are on the menu at every meal. Fried chicken is a staple. Mr. Van Dyke, a man whose expansive physique betrays an unbridled passion for food, admits that he is a fried-chicken fanatic. "I order fried chicken everywhere I go, even in a Chinese restaurant," he says. "So, I was fussy when I developed the recipe for the fried chicken we serve here." It is grand and true southern-fried chicken, nearly greaseless, but with a well-spiced crust that has a luscious texture, shattering at first bite and infusing the meat within with flavor.

Of course, mashed potatoes are almost always on the menu, and they are as good as mashed potatoes can be. One day in the midst of the lunch hour we looked into the kitchen and saw head cook Ann Lowe mashing a tub of them by hand. It is hard work to plow through so big a mountain of potatoes, but such results cannot be achieved by mashing potatoes with a machine: dense, buttery swells of ivory-hued spud— a significant presence on a plate.

Another dish that requires plenty of hand labor is collard greens. Before being cooked with ham hocks and salt pork, the greens must be washed and rewashed several times. Because they cook down, losing volume as they absorb the porky flavors in their boiling water, vast amounts of raw collards must be cleaned to meet the daily demand. Mr. Van Dyke, a self-taught cook, recalled the time he thought he figured out a way to automate the process. He put an armload of collard greens in his washing machine. "All I can tell you is this," he said. "Never use the spin cycle. The greens came out clean, but we had little bits of them on our clothes for weeks." Now Blue Willow collards are washed the old-fashioned way, by hand, before they are cooked until limp, but still firm enough to provide a bit of tooth resistance, then chopped into leafy little pieces about the size of postage stamps. They are an enticing green with a unique not-quite-bitter bite. As one customer, apparently a stranger to Dixie cooking, considers them in their serving pan, Mr. Van Dyke looks over her shoulder at the glistening leaves and advises, "You *must* try collards. You'll either love them or you will hate them, and if you decide you love them, you will just have to stay with us in the South."

The signature dish of the inn is fried green tomatoes, which are always offered with bright red tomato chutney in a nearby bowl. The tomatoes are served year 'round, shipped in from wherever they are currently green, sometimes Mexico or California. They are then sliced by hand. (When we were introduced to the Van Dykes' grandson, his hand was bandaged; Mrs. Van Dyke referred to his injury as a "green-tomato thumb.") The slices are battered and fried in hot oil, resulting in a crisp, crunchy disc with juicy insides just tart enough to balance the richness of their crust. The chutney is sweet, pickly stuff, the tomatoes' ideal companion, and also mighty tasty when spooned onto green beans, pole beans, shoepeg corn, or collards.

Distinguished southern food is what motivates customers to travel long distances to feast at the Blue Willow Inn, but the experience of coming to Social Circle through the Georgia countryside is a joy itself, especially in the spring, when the dogwoods, wisteria, and cherry blossoms are in bloom. The main street of Social Circle has scarcely changed from a century ago. At Claude T. Wiley Co. general store, an ancient wood-floored emporium with shelves of dry goods, groceries, and knickknacks, we purchased a lovely ladies' hanky for fifty-nine cents and, in the nearby grocery store we found a butcher's case featuring every pig part but the oink. In the center of the street is a flower-ringed monument erected by the Social Circle Garden Club explaining the origin of the town's name: "A group of men sitting in a circle, having their usual drink, were approached by a stranger. He was invited to join the group. Pleased with such hospitality, he exclaimed, 'This is surely a social circle.' . . . "

Social, indeed! The range of people who consider the Blue Willow Inn their kind of place is astounding. Visitors from 153 foreign countries have signed the guest book. Some celebrating customers arrive wearing silk gowns or business suits; others come in shorts and T-shirts with flip-flops on their feet; on weekdays, local workmen eat lunch in their overalls. Harley-Davidson clubs have dined here, outfitted in leather and denim, as have garden clubs of ladies wearing pastel pantsuits and white patent-leather shoes. Everyone is welcome, with only a few exceptions. Once, when a young man arrived with a four-letter word on his T-shirt, he was asked to leave. And Billie Van Dyke, only half-kidding, says, "When people come in looking for low-fat food, we tell them to go eat at the hospital."

Tomato Chutney for Fried Green Tomatoes

1 14-ounce can whole tomatoes

1 cup light-brown sugar

$^1/_2$ cup sugar

2 cups finely chopped green pepper

1 cup finely chopped onion

2 tablespoons ketchup

2–10 drops of Tabasco sauce, to taste

1 teaspoon black pepper

1. In a heavy saucepan, stir together all the ingredients. Cook at a simmer, about 2 hours, stirring frequently, until thickened.

2. Cool. Serve with fried green tomatoes. Will keep 2 weeks, refrigerated.

Makes about 4 cups.

Fried Green Tomatoes

2 eggs

$1^1/_2$ cups buttermilk

$1^1/_2$ cups self-rising flour

1 teaspoon salt

1 teaspoon black pepper

3 large green tomatoes, cut into $^1/_4$-inch slices

Vegetable oil, for frying

1. In a broad bowl, mix the eggs and buttermilk. Whisk in 1 tablespoon flour, $^1/_2$ teaspoon salt, and $^1/_2$ teaspoon pepper. Soak tomato slices in mixture.

2. Whisk together the remaining flour, salt, and pepper.

3. Heat about 1 inch oil to 350°F in a heavy skillet.

4. Dredge tomato slices, one at a time, in seasoned flour, shaking off any excess. Fry in uncrowded batches in the hot oil. (Slices should not overlap as they cook.) Fry each until crisp. Transfer to paper towel to drain. Salt to taste.

5. Serve with tomato chutney.

Makes 4–6 servings.

Bon Ton Mini Mart

HENDERSON, KENTUCKY

*A*quarter century ago, when George Markham was a student at Henderson County High School in western Kentucky, he fell in love with fried chicken. Along with his classmates, he regularly feasted at a restaurant just across the street from campus called the Colonels' Lair. It was named for the school's football team, known as the Colonels, and it was run by a man named Bill Koch, whom everyone called Bilko, because that's the way he pronounced his name. All who remember those days agree that Bilko made the best fried chicken anywhere. In the state where Harland Sanders began a fried-chicken empire based on the secret recipe he used in the kitchen of his service station/café, such judgments are not made lightly.

Bilko's chicken was different from Colonel Sanders'. It was infused with a powerpacked spice marinade of cayenne and garlic that penetrated to the bone, and it was encased with a dark, brittle crust nearly as salty as a potato chip. Dark or light meat, Bilko's chicken parts delivered a taste thrill like none other. "He dinged around with different spices for a long time," recalls Donna King, who worked with the Koch family at the Colonels' Lair for eleven years. "When he first started making it, it was really, really hot. People would cry when they ate it . . . but they liked it and wanted more! He finally got the cayenne pepper down to where it was supposed to be, and I guess we sold a million pieces of chicken."

In 1983, the Koch family pulled up stakes and moved to Las Vegas, Nevada, where Bilko cooked and served his chicken in a small casino off the strip. Henderson, Kentucky, was left chickenless.

A tragedy happened in 1996. On their way to a family reunion, the Koch family car was hit by a semitrailer truck, and all but Bilko's daughter Cheri, traveling in another vehicle behind, were killed.

Meanwhile, back in Henderson, a woman named Mary Spence was

transforming Bon Ton Mini Mart on old Highway 41, south of town. When she opened the convenience store in the mid-1970s, the plan was to sell kitchen staples, household goods, John Deere caps, and basic automotive supplies, such as motor oil and wiper blades. Soon, she installed a few breakfast tables and started offering biscuits and gravy in the morning. Local farm workers and construction crews enjoyed eating at Bon Ton so much that noonday meals were added to the menu, and by the early 1990s, Bon Ton was known for its fine plate lunch.

Bon Ton's cook is former Colonels' Lair employee Donna King, and good fried chicken was part of her repertoire. But it was not Bilko's chicken. "I didn't know how to make it!" Donna confesses with some embarrassment. "I knew the formula at one time. I had it. But then I lost it. I forgot!"

When George Markham bought Bon Ton Mini Mart seven years ago, one of the first things he did was to take out all the shelves and put in more tables. "People were coming in hungry to eat, but having to wait," he says. "It would be one hundred degrees outside or twenty below zero, and we had only four booths, which wasn't nearly enough. So I said, 'This is kind of silly,' and I bought more tables. I changed the place from fifty percent restaurant to one hundred percent. Now, all that's left from those days of the mini-mart are the work gloves, candy, and bags of chips."

When George bought Bon Ton, he was familiar with the food business—he had been a meat cutter and had sold groceries—but running a restaurant was new to him. So, he was delighted that Donna was there when he arrived. "She kinda came with the furniture," he says with a loving smile. "She knew a whole lot more about running a restaurant than I did."

Donna is a go-getter. Although the doors to the Bon Ton open every morning at four, her day begins at 1:00 AM, when she comes in to start breakfast, bake cakes, and cook vegetables for lunch. "What we do in this kitchen is not opening a can. It is *cooking*," she says, referring to such labor-intensive dishes as fried apples, hash-brown casserole, and escalloped potatoes, as well as big, sheet-cake desserts made from fresh bananas and strawberries. "As a child growing up on a farm outside of Henderson, I learned how to put food on the table for my family of eight brothers and sisters. We had our own chickens—raised them and killed them and plucked them and fried them in lard."

With George at the helm of Bon Ton Mini Mart, Donna saw an opportunity to remake the former convenience store. She started with the walls. "When I came to work here, it was all wood paneling," she says. "Dark and gloomy. I felt I needed to lighten it up. So I started painting. I had a color mixed, a pretty one, but once I got it on the walls it looked a whole lot pinker than it did in the can. George walked in one morning and said, 'What the heck are you doing with these walls?' I said, 'Just wait till I get through. You'll like it. I found curtains that matched perfect, and a nice blue for an accent. I still get teased about it

by the construction crews who come in here to eat. They give me a hard time about the pink. I tell them, 'Just be happy. It could have been a red room or a green one!' And you know something? This pink-and-blue combination is really very relaxing. A lot of your rest homes have gone to these colors because they actually provide comfort to the patients. It's a nice calm atmosphere to start the day."

About four years ago, Donna and George got to reminiscing about Bilko's chicken, and thinking how good it would be to have some again. Donna had remained friends with the family when they moved away, and had kept in touch with the surviving daughter after the accident. One morning when George walked in, Donna said, "Send me to Las Vegas. I'll get the fried-chicken recipe."

Cheri Koch and Donna King mixed two hundred pounds of spice mix according to Bilko's original formula. "I arrived from Nevada at the St. Louis airport at five o'clock in the morning with nobody to help me and all these buckets of seasoning to lift," Donna remembers. "I didn't know what I was going to do. But somehow I ended up with it in my car and brought it home. I did it for Bon Ton, but I also did it to help Cheri and to keep her Daddy's memory alive. I know how he worked his heart out on that chicken."

Bon Ton Mini Mart is so small and out of the way that many residents of Henderson have no idea that it exists, but old-timers who remember the Colonels' Lair found out about it fast enough and spread the word. Now, chicken lovers from all over western Kentucky have made the pilgrimage to the south side of Henderson a regular habit. "One of the ladies who comes in asked me what I put in it," Donna chuckles. "The lady says, 'It's a drug, I know it's a drug because I have to have it every day.' I tell her there are no drugs in it, just spices, and she says, 'I am addicted to your chicken!' I tell her, 'Yes, I know. That's what I made it for.'"

To most of those who have never tasted it, the first bite is astonishing. Like aged country ham, it might seem almost too intense: spicy, salty, crunchy all at once. But as tongue shock settles, tastebuds crave more, and after a few bites, one's whole world very quickly shrinks to nothing other than this amazing fried chicken and the rapturous necessity of devouring every edible morsel of it.

Bon-Ton-Style Fried Chicken

Bilko's spice mix is a closely guarded secret, but Donna King shared with us its fundamental ingredients, as well as the basic principle of a long marinade—at least twenty-four hours. During that time, she explained, blood seems to be drawn from the meat, allowing for a briefer frying time, and resulting in the juiciest possible chicken with flavor insinuated into every fiber. She also explained that the pieces must rest five or ten minutes and "get doughy" after being dredged in spiced flour, and that pure vegetable shortening will insure it is greaseless.

Because of limited refrigeration space, Bon Ton can keep only one case of chicken parts marinating, meaning that supplies sometimes run out. "You want to see some angry customers?" George Markham asks. Come here one day at noon when there isn't any chicken. You've never heard such squawking!"

MARINADE

1 quart water

2 tablespoons salt

2 teaspoons cayenne pepper

2 teaspoons garlic powder

1 teaspoon Accent

1¹/₂ teaspoons white pepper

1 tablespoon soy sauce

2 teaspoons Worcestershire sauce

4 bone-in, skin-on breasts, 4 thighs, and 4 drumsticks, washed

Vegetable oil, for frying

Stir all the seasonings into the water, mashing the garlic powder and pepper so that they don't clump. Find a bowl just big enough to hold the chicken, and cover the chicken with marinade. Cover bowl and refrigerate twenty-four hours, moving the chicken parts around once or twice.

SPICED FLOUR

3 cups all-purpose flour

1 tablespoon salt

1 teaspoon garlic powder

1 teaspoon Accent

1 teaspoon cayenne pepper

1 teaspoon white pepper

1. Mix all ingredients.

2. Heat about 2 inches vegetable oil to 365–375°F in a deep cast-iron pot or skillet.

3. Pull the chicken piece by piece from the marinade and dredge it directly in the seasoned flour. Set it on a baking sheet or aluminum foil, 5–10 minutes.

4. Cook chicken in hot oil, 20–25 minutes, turning each piece a few times, so it cooks evenly and turns golden brown.

5. Drain on a brown paper bag or wire rack and serve.

Makes 6 servings.

C&K Barbecue

*E*very city in America has its own favorite edible oddities, from the well-known (gumbo in New Orleans) to the obscure (runzas in Lincoln, Nebraska), but none has so many or such strange culinary passions as St. Louis.

Some cognoscenti know about its toasted ravioli, the crisp-crusted dumplings originally made popular in the Italian neighborhood known as The Hill, and serious sweet tooths are respectful of the amazing concrete (an ultrathick milk shake) made by Ted Drewes' custard stand, but there are several St. Louis food specialties so deeply ingrained in what must be called the city's underground gastronomy that even many local food authorities know little or nothing about them. Brains, for example, are a specialty of at least a half-dozen otherwise inconspicuous taverns in town. They are breaded and deep fried and served with mustard on rye bread, and the barkeep/cooks who make them vie to earn a reputation among tavern folk for the best brains (a title earned by fluffiness and flavor). One of St. Louis's culinary mysteries is that virtually every chop-suey joint in town (and the city is filled with them) lists on its menu a sandwich known as the St. Paul: a patty of egg foo yong on Wonder bread with lettuce, tomato, and a slice of cheese! We once spent a week talking to Chinese cooks, local food historians, and newspaper reporters trying to find out where this Chinese-American invention came from and how it got named St. Paul, and no one had a clue.

The most delicious of all the city's eccentric likings is snoots, as made by Daryle Brantley of C&K Barbecue out on Jennings Station Road near the highway. Years ago, when we were eating our way around town, a tipster in another barbecue restaurant first told us about Daryle's magnificent snoots. We dared not assume what we later learned to be the truth: Snoots are snouts, snouts of pigs to be precise, that are baked until crisp, broken into bite-sized pieces, then refried until they attain a succulence that causes them literally to melt in your mouth. Bathed in Daryle Brantley's nuclear-strength barbecue sauce and served in a most unmanageable configuration between two puny pieces of white bread, a snoot sandwich is a delicacy that no hungry—and adventurous—visitor to the Gateway City can afford to miss.

"Snoots go way back," Darryle explained to us one afternoon as we stood with him in the C&K kitchen, its air perfumed by the sweet, smoky aroma of pit-cooked pig. "We ate snoots when I was a boy. We ate *every part* of that pig! Every part but the squeal. We had to, because we were poor and we couldn't afford to have a ham or a beef tenderloin. Now I see people come through these doors who, if they wanted to, could be eating filet mignon three times a day. But that fancy steak doesn't do it for them; it's not like what their mamma made. So they buy a snoot plate here for $4.75, and they are happy!"

We must confess that Daryle is a little peeved at us for having told the world about his snoots ten years ago in our guidebook *Goodfood*. He has a lot of fun introducing travelers from all over the country to snoots, but even he has to admit that for many people, pig proboscises are a not easily acquired taste, and he really does want visitors to know that there are many other more accessible soul-food smokehouse specialties on his menu, such as whole racks of ribs, hot links, and whole chickens. We love Daryle's barbecued pork ribs, and the sauce he makes is a Missouri masterpiece but, the last time we visited, we were struck by yet another oddity on the menu, listed with no extraneous adjective or description: "Pig Ear."

We ordered pig ear, expecting something that, like snoots, had been transformed from its familiar anatomical shape into something that looked more like normal food. What arrived was astonishing: two slices of bread with one large and very recognizable whole ear of a pig sandwiched between them garnished with mustard and pickle! We picked up the sandwich, the flesh-colored meat hanging limp within the bread and honestly, it was one of the most difficult bites we ever attempted. Once we surrendered to the challenge, it was tasty, sweet and moist, like loin of pork, but the most amazing thing about it was its tenderness. It was soft as warm butter.

"Daryle," we asked. "Ears are cartilage, which should be tough. Why is this so tender?"

"Boiling," he answered. "I do it just the way my mother did it, and she boiled ears all afternoon."

We were skeptical, not believing that boiling could make anything once so tough turn so tender. Daryle saw our disbelief, and stepped close to confide in us a culinary truth with the same conviction that a priest might use to give his parishioner the Word of God. "Water works miracles," Daryle said. "It can cut a Grand Canyon, it can move a mountain, it can make grass grow in the valley. You *know* it can make a pig ear tender."

Snoot Sauce

Rest assured: This classic Midwest-style barbecue sauce tastes fine on ordinary cuts of pork, such as tenderloin or ribs. It's also great on beef or chicken. Use it to baste the meat as it cooks, then serve a cupful on the side for dipping.

4 cloves garlic, minced	4 tablespoons Worcestershire sauce
4 tablespoons butter	1 tablespoon soy sauce
1 tablespoon lemon juice	1–4 teaspoons Tabasco sauce, to taste
½ cup minced red onion	
2 cups cider vinegar	2 teaspoons salt
2 cups tomato juice	1 teaspoon coarse-ground black pepper
½ cup dark brown sugar	

1. In a cast-iron skillet, sauté the garlic in the butter until it is soft but not yet browned. Add the remaining ingredients and bring to the lowest possible simmer, then lower heat a notch or two. Cook, uncovered, 1 hour, stirring frequently and keeping the temperature just below a boil.

2. Store in refrigerator. Serve warm.

Makes a generous quart.

Café Poca Cosa

TUCSON, ARIZONA

S uzana Davila grew up in restaurants. Her father, Luis Davila, ran one in Guaymas, Sonora, Mexico, when she was a little girl, and she used to help him fold the napkins and arrange the silverware, but he always warned her that, when she grew up, she should stay away from the business. "Too iffy, too day-to-day," he said to her. As a young woman, Suzana moved north to Tucson, Arizona, where she became an interior designer, and was known for the southwestern panache of the homes and gardens she styled for the city's elite. That job often put her in the media spotlight and, because she is six feet tall and drop-dead gorgeous, with raven hair and a willowy figure, she also started working as a fashion model.

Prior to studio sessions in the old downtown part of Tucson, Suzana often had her morning coffee in a restaurant called La Indita on South Scott Avenue next to the Federal Building. It was a minuscule shoebox of a café, with room for about twenty customers at a time. In 1986, when La Indita suddenly went up for sale, Suzana bought it on a whim. Despite her father's advice, she felt a powerful yearning that could not be denied. "I love to cook," she says. "I needed to cook. Here was my chance. I knew I had to take it. I went in there, painted the place all bright colors, brought in Mexican furniture, named it Poca Cosa (Little Thing), and waited for a customer."

At the time, downtown Tucson was undergoing drastic renovation. Whole streets were blocked off and torn up. Although the point of all the work was to make the city core more attractive for shoppers, the construction turned it into a temporary dead zone. "For months, I had no customers whatsoever," Suzana recalls. However, if there is one quality this woman radiates (beyond the benign wizardry she shares with so many great chefs), it is resourcefulness. Nothing gets in her way. "What

I did each day before lunch was go outside and whistle to the workers repairing the streets, calling them over to ask what they wanted to eat. They told me and I made it for them. Gradually, the word got out, and, although in those days few people came downtown for dinner, I developed a good business for breakfast and lunch. My father, who had retired, came to help, told me everything I was doing wrong, and showed me how to do it right." In those days, regulars frequently pitched in by bussing their own tables, and it became a custom among loyal friends of the establishment to ignore the menu on the blackboard and simply walk back to the tiny kitchen to see what Suzana and her father had cooking on the stove that day.

After three years, Suzana craved a bigger canvas, and her reputation as a culinary artist had interested a number of financiers who offered to support her in a more deluxe location somewhere in the foothills, but she resisted. "I like it here downtown," she says. "It is so much more sociable. You can eat, you can stroll, you can see the art and enjoy the city. In February for the Gem Show (the world's largest) and Fiesta de los Vaqueros (one of the West's classic rodeos), this is the only place to be. And during the Mariachi Festival (April), it is crazy. Wonderfully crazy. How could I leave all this?"

When space opened up at the Park Inn, a large hotel a half block from the Café Poca Cosa, Suzana Davila found her destiny. For Suzana, who knows Tucson history, the location was a magic one, formerly the Santa Rita Hotel. A five-story mission-style palace favored by cattlemen, movie stars, and high rollers from around the world, the Santa Rita had served as a focal point for Tucson society from 1904 into the years after World War II. Much of the old building was demolished in 1972, long after its heyday, but many natives still think of this real estate as the Santa Rita's piece of town; that high-toned reputation is a legacy Suzana Davila tenaciously upholds.

She cooks different things every day. Customers make requests for her picadillo or pork roast stuffed with plums, and chipotle chilies with tamarind; a waiter or a member of the kitchen staff will be inspired by a stash of hibiscus flowers and remind her of a dish she makes called *chicken tropicale*, flavored with hibiscus, pineapple, orange, lemon juice, and peppercorns; a farmer will arrive early in the morning with a basket of smoky pasilla chilies she can use to make quesadillas with a breathtaking wallop; whenever rare *cuitlacoche* can be harvested, the lusty corncob fungus is mixed with corn kernels, tomato bits, lots of garlic, olive oil, and cheese and served atop steamed-soft corn tortillas.

"My cooking is from all over Mexico," Suzana says. "I use thirty different kinds of chile, many of them supplied by friends from their farms and backyards. Beef is as popular in Sonora, Mexico, as it is in Tucson. For the *carne asada*, I make a *salsa de molcajete* (the *molcajete* is the traditional mortar and pestle made of porous lava stone) of yellow peppers, serranos, tomato, and garlic." This salsa makes the meat into a luscious pot roast, thickened with avocados and redolent of wine. Hot chipotle chilies are used to flavor grilled steak strips; *carne asada barbacoa* is steeped in beer and seasoned with chilies and bay leaves.

"Beef is local; but *molé* comes from deeper down in Mexico," the chef explains; and there are always at least a few *molés* written on the blackboard. *Pollo en molé negro* is like the bittersweet *molé* most of us have sampled—a strange blend of chile's heat and chocolate's richness, with cinnamon somewhere between the two; Suzana's version is miraculous, spangled with sesame seeds and teetering in perfect balance between the provocation of pepper pods and the sensuality of cocoa. The thick, inky sauce pervades the chicken and gives every bite a resonance that both stimulates and satisfies an appetite like no other food. *Molé verde* is as verdant as the *negro* is earthy, with an exotic herbal hue. And there is *molé rojo*, made of lighter red chilies and crushed tortillas, similar to *negro*, but not so ominously dark.

Poca Cosa Chicken Molé Verde

Molé verde, *which Oaxacans know simply as* verde, *is loaded with cilantro and* tomatillos; *taking a cue from around Cuernavaca where pumpkins grow, Suzana adds plenty of pumpkin seeds. Use it to cosset pieces of cooked chicken, pork, or turkey. (Pumpkin seeds can be found at health-food stores.)*

1 cup sesame seeds

1/2 cup hulled raw pumpkin seeds

1/3 cup hulled pistachio nuts

1/3 cup blanched whole almonds

4 large cloves garlic

3 fresh poblano chilies, with seeds, chopped

4 fresh serrano chilies, chopped

1 1/2 cups tomatillos, husks removed, chopped

1 large bunch cilantro, washed and chopped

6 corn tortillas, browned and broken into pieces

1 cup shredded iceberg lettuce

4 cups chicken broth

3 tablespoons safflower oil

3 pounds cooked chicken or pork

1. In an ungreased frying pan, toast the sesame seeds over medium heat, stirring constantly until they turn dark, about 8 minutes. Turn them onto a platter to cool. In the same pan, heat the pumpkin seeds, 2–3 minutes, long enough for them to puff up but not darken. Set them aside with the sesame seeds. Toast the pistachios and almonds, 2–3 minutes and add them to the seed–nut mixture.

2. Put the garlic, chilies, tomatillos, cilantro, tortillas, and lettuce in a blender. Process with just enough chicken broth to form a rugged paste. Add the seed–nut mixture and blend enough to mix well, but not smooth.

3. Put the mixture in a saucepan with the safflower oil. Cook over medium heat, stirring frequently, 12 minutes. Add chicken broth if necessary, the sauce should be quite thick and pasty.

4. Add cooked pork or chicken, and cook over medium heat, 5–10 minutes.

5. Serve with corn tortillas, rice, and beans.

Makes 6–8 servings.

Carol's Calico Kitchen

LEXINGTON, MINNESOTA

*C*ountry cafés are like country pies: the ones that are homely on the outside tend to be the most delicious. So, when we spotted Carol's Calico Kitchen by the side of the road, where it adjoins Ray's Small Engine Repair, our hearts soared. We had been tipped off by Grace and Andy Gibas, long-time residents, who wrote to say that Carol's Calico Kitchen was our kind of place. Wow, were they correct! And, as is true about every great restaurant, whether four-star or simply foursquare, its greatness flows from the vision and talents of a single individual. In this case, that individual is Carol Brown.

Carol is fanatical about the food that comes from her kitchen. Her particular mania is that everything served be homemade, from scratch. "I waitressed here long ago when this was called the Lexington Café," she recalls. "I felt so bad serving store-bought bread that I would heat it up before bringing it to a table. I always dreamed that if I ever had a restaurant of my own, I would bake the bread just like my grandparents did on their farm in the North Country."

The Calico Kitchen menu is replete with reminders of Carol's philosophy:

> *We do not use any sugar in our dough, only honey!!*
> *We make our own jams and syrup*
> *For our salads we do our own dressings*
> *We boil, peel, grate, chop, and mash all our potatoes*
> *Our pancakes are made from scratch with real buttermilk*

Although the menu notes that the biscuits are *homemade*, it does not mention that their savory flavor is owed to the fact that Carol's dough is made the old-fashioned way, with lard. The result is a fluffy biscuit with a creamy complexion; it is a special pleasure at breakfast to spread out the fingers of one hand to encircle one of these big boys on the plate, to gingerly twist off its top, and to lay a sphere of butter down and watch it melt as aromatic baking-powder–biscuit steam wafts above the plate. Carol also uses lard to make pie crusts that are lush and flaky.

Fresh produce is her siren song. "I am not a vegetarian, but I am into vegetables," she says. "When I see bunches of nice, big beets or good green beans at the market, I buy all I can and cook them up to serve with supper." For her renowned rhubarb cream pie, she gets rhubarb from spring into August from a local man's garden. Starting midsummer, corn on the cob is a regular companion to almost every dinner.

Carol's personality is everywhere in the restaurant, which she describes as "just an old place I've fluffed." Her fluffing style is flamboyantly feminine, including flowered wallpaper, enormous silver and lavender metallic-fabric window swags intertwined with honeysuckle vines and silken roses, and sentimental prints on the wall showing cherubic children and faithful dogs. "Some of the men who regularly eat here had a fit when they saw me start to fluff," Carol recalls, referring to the blue-collar crowd who are her regulars. "They said, 'Now, don't make it all lacy and girly.' I said to them, 'Boys, you've been complaining about how bad this place looks for years now. So, be quiet and eat!'" The contrast between her decorative flourishes and the rugged look of so many of the workmen who come for breakfast gives the scene in the dining room a new-world Victorian charm. Although the building itself is ramshackle ("I've got a supply of buckets to arrange for leaks when it rains!" Carol says), the ambiance is relentlessly civilized.

Carol is a religious person, a nonprofessional faith healer who sometimes conveys her God's strength by laying on of hands for customers with aching backs or workplace injuries; above the swinging kitchen doors that lead to the kitchen, a wood plaque says *Give Us This Day Our Daily Bread*. A devotional portrait of Jesus Christ hangs in a place of honor near the cash register. Even bigger than Jesus is a picture of a mortal man from whom Carol derives much earthly verve and inspiration: Tony Little. A life-sized poster shows the musclebound, hyperthyroid infomercial pitchman with a rhetorical caption, *Where Does Tony Little Get His Energy?* The answer can be found on a nearby shelf of Tony Little-endorsed vitamins and Eternal Energy-brand food supplements that Carol sells.

For our energy source, we prefer to start the day with one of Carol Brown's breakfasts, preferably hash. Varieties of hash include roast beef, corned beef, and spicy Italian sausage, each of which is cut into a chunky jumble and served on a bale of crisp hash browns. Hash and all egg breakfasts are accompanied by white or whole wheat toast, sliced extra thick, and jam made from a mix of raspberries, blueberries, straw-berries, honey, and orange-spice seasonings. Sweet rolls, made from potato-flour dough, are immense—a full six inches in diameter and two inches tall—served in a deep pool of warm caramel sauce with a quar-ter cup of whipped butter on the side. (Warning: The day's supply of caramel rolls is often gone well before noon.)

There is no mistaking Calico Kitchen pancakes for ones made from a mix. These tawny beauties are as wide as their plate, lightweight and tender with a buttermilk tang, served with a ramekin full of butter and a pitcher of syrup. We were especially smitten by the sensuously tex-tured raisin-walnut cakes, as well as by the Amish potato cakes that are made from leftover mashed potatoes whipped silky-smooth with eggs and flour, then fried in butter until their crust turns gold. The potato pancakes are considered breakfast (they're served with syrup), but Carol's is the sort of place that serves breakfast any time. We imagine these potato cakes would make an ideal side dish for a plate of roast pork at supper.

The day's baked goods are displayed each morning near the cash register where, on your way toward a seat at lunchtime, you will vow to leave room for a square of apple-walnut cake, a dark, moist pastry served under a mantle of that fine caramel sauce, either à la mode or topped with a cloud of whipped cream. Among the daily bakery reper-toire is a loaf that Carol calls fritter bread, which is laced with chopped apples and cinnamon sugar. Dipped in egg batter, slices of this sweet bread become fabulous French toast.

Although she is adamant about not serving anything ready made or artificial, Carol Brown makes no lofty claims for the recipes she uses. "This is just regular food," she explains. "Regular food that regular people like to eat. My recipes come from childhood and from church cookbooks." Her most popular meal, on the menu every day, is roast-turkey dinner. This is a $6.95 plate of moist white and dark slices, sage-scented stuffing, and a great glob of mashed potatoes all smothered with gravy, sided by a vegetable, a cup of cranberry relish, white or wheat bread, and—if it's Thanksgiving or if Carol is in a holiday mood—a serving of candied-yam casserole veined with melted brown sugar. Nothing could be more "regular."

At one time, a few years ago, Carol thought it might be a good idea to replace the regular spaghetti with angel hair pasta. "I never heard such an uproar!" she recalls. "From the local boys, of course. They didn't like those skinny noodles with their meatballs, and they were not shy about complaining." So, Carol brought back regulation-size spaghetti and now offers both kinds of pasta on the menu. "I listen to my customers," she says. "They may pour concrete or sweep floors out there but, in here, they are my kings and queens." Carol recently deleted rye bread from her daily roster because it became too time-consuming to separate leftover rye from white and wheat when she was cutting croutons for the salads . . . and several of her regular "boys" cannot abide the taste of the caraway seeds in the rye. "Of course, I can't listen to *everything* they say," Carol adds. "If I did, I'd serve nothing but stacks of pancakes in the morning and meatloaf and mashed potatoes all day long!"

In March 2000, a night fire gutted Carol's Calico Kitchen. There were no injuries, but the restaurant has closed, pending rebuilding or possible relocation.

Amish Chicken

As far as Carol Brown knows, there are no communities of the Plain People near Lexington, but Amish chicken, for which she found the recipe in a self-published cookbook, has become a weekly staple at her café. "It's so crazy simple!" she declares. The long cooking time in a cream bath makes the meat fall-off-the-bone tender. It is a supremely mild meal, which we have now added to our repertoire of adult nursery food, for those occasions when only the gentlest fare can fulfill the need for total comfort.

1 cup all-purpose flour

2 teaspoons garlic powder

2 teaspoons seasoned salt

2 teaspoons white pepper

1 teaspoon paprika

$^{1}/_{3}$ cup finely chopped parsley

9 chicken quarters, washed and patted dry

$1^{1}/_{2}$ cups cream

$1^{1}/_{2}$ cups water

1. Preheat oven to 350°F.

2. Mix together flour, garlic powder, seasoned salt, white pepper, paprika, and parsley.

3. Dredge chicken in flour mixture, knock off excess flour, and place it skin side up in a deep baking pan or large Dutch oven. Mix the cream and water together and pour over the chicken. Bake, 2 hours, or until skin is crisp. Serve with stuffing and mashed potatoes.

Makes 9 servings.

Rhubarb Cream Pie

From spring through the height of summer, this pie is made from rhubarb, delivered fresh to the restaurant from a local garden. For a month or so after rhubarb season, it is made with extra rhubarb that Carol freezes.

Rolled-out dough for a double-crust 9-inch pie

2 egg yolks

1 cup sugar

1 cup cream

2 tablespoons all-purpose flour

Pinch of nutmeg

2 cups chopped rhubarb

1. Preheat oven to 350°F.

2. Line a 9-inch pie pan with half the rolled-out dough.

3. Mix egg yolks, sugar, cream, flour, and nutmeg. Stir in the chopped rhubarb. Pour into dough-lined pan. Cover it with the remaining dough, trimming and crimping edges and cutting vents in the top for steam to escape.

4. Bake, 1 hour.

Makes one 9-inch pie.

Clark's Outpost

TIOGA, TEXAS

*I*n Texas, in the late 1960s, wholesale garment salesman Warren Clark devised a shrewd tactic to lure buyers to the hotel room in which he displayed his line of clothes. He went to Sonny Bryan's restaurant in Dallas and bought a whole barbecued brisket and a whole smoked ham, which he carried back to his room and set up on hot plates to keep warm. Through his open hotel room door, the powerful aroma of hot meats wafted through the hallways and into the elevators. Buyers came to him in hordes and they ate plenty, but Mr. Clark didn't sell much merchandise, because the clothes, sharing space with such fine barbecue, soon began to smell like smokehouse delicacies themselves. Still, Warren Clark didn't mind. He enjoyed sharing the food with friends and associates, and he particularly relished all the time he spent at Sonny Bryan's, where he devoted days apprenticing with the master learning to turn raw briskets into beef ambrosia.

A quarter of a century ago, when he realized his heart wasn't in the clothing business, Warren Clark gave it up to realize his dream: to live in the farmland of North Texas and run a barbecue restaurant like that of his mentor, Sonny Bryan. Mr. Clark died four years ago but, now that he is gone, his widow, Nancy Ann Clark, carries on his enterprise with the resolve of a crusader on a sacred mission. As his partner for all those years, she knows exactly how to run the restaurant, which, although seemingly casual, is a precisely orchestrated gastronomic experience. Nothing about a meal at Clark's is accidental. For example, sauce for the barbecue is presented in recycled Grolsch beer bottles—an apparently offhand touch, unless you note that the bottles are kept warm in a *bain-marie* until the moment they are served. Each rickety table, covered with green-checked oilcloth, is equipped with a three-bottle battery of accoutrements essential for enjoyment of Clark's Wild West cuisine: hot sauce, pickled "sport" peppers, and wooden toothpicks.

Clark's renown was built on beef. In the early days, that's nearly all there was on the menu, and it was prepared the Sonny Bryan way. "There are no secrets," Sonny used to tell Warren. "There is just time. Time and smoke." Briskets are put into smokers over smoldering green hickory or pecan wood ("Mesquite burns too hot; oak has a bad taste," Nancy Ann explains), where they bask in the pungent smoke at 175 degrees for a few hours, then are turned down to a superslow 150 degrees to cook for three days more. Nothing is put onto the beef as it cooks—no seasonings, no sauces, no marinade. The only trick is to have a hunk of brisket with a good layer of fat on top, so that as the smoke drifts through it, drippings infuse every fiber of the meat. The result is elemental food: beef and smoke laced together in an exquisite harmony that words cannot convey. Rimmed with a crust of smoky black, each slice is so supple that the gentlest fork pressure separates a mouthful. The warm barbecue sauce, supplied on the side in those beer bottles, is dark, spicy, and provocatively sweet.

Nancy Ann Clark, herself a refugee from the garment business, has become a fount of wisdom about Texas gastronomic ways. "Calf fries are a lost art," she declares, referring to the most tender part of a young male bovine, the old prairie delicacy euphemistically known as *swinging beef* or *prairie oysters* or, on jocular menus, *tendergroin*. Only one butcher in Fort Worth is considered good enough to supply calf fries fine enough to suit Clark's standards. "You buy your calf fries somewhere else, you might get that big old bull meat, which is tough. We use only the small ones—we skin them, we cut them, and we fry them to order; we go through so many that I had to tell our butcher to start accumulating fries as the spring approaches, because he doesn't slaughter in the summer and we cannot go that long without them." Clark's cooks up about two thousand pounds of the delicate organ meat each year. Fried crisp, but melting-soft inside, they are cattle-country treats served with rugged pan gravy on the side.

To go with the platters of meat, Clark's offers a slew of country-style side dishes, ranging from classic crisp-fried okra and old-time red beans to jalapeño-spiked black-eyed peas, and a marvelous oddity, French-fried corn on the cob. Lengths of corn, unbattered and unadorned, are dipped in hot oil for about a minute, just long enough for the kernels to cook and begin to caramelize. The process yields corn that is quite soft, with a mere veil of a crust, and astoundingly sweet. Each piece is served with a black-smith's nail stuck in each end to serve as holders. If you really like the taste of collard greens, you'll love Clark's. The heavy leaves are served in a glossy wet heap, so radiant with green-vegetable flavor that we invariably congratulate ourselves for our healthy eating habits as we fork them up.

In many otherwise exemplary roadhouse restaurants, dessert is an afterthought, at best. Not at Clark's, though, where grand, parchment-crusted coconut and chocolate pies are made every morning by waitress Patty Seyler, who has perfected the art of building towering meringues that are more ethereal than clouds in heaven. "We need Patty because she is a seven-day-a-week pie maker," Nancy Ann Clark says. "You can't serve yesterday's meringue: It isn't light the way meringue should be."

Despite success and renown, Clark's has remained assertively rustic. Much of its charm is its location in the Red River country town of Tioga, the population of which has more than doubled since the restaurant opened—from 300 to 625. Still little more than a farmland crossroads, Tioga's ancient main street—named Gene Autry Drive, in honor of its famous native son—consists of a tack shop, a realtor's office, and a cat-fish parlor. Around the corner, at the junction of Gene Autry Drive and Highway 377, Clark's is a small agglomeration of joined-together wood buildings, surrounded by a gravel parking lot and stacks of wood for the smoker, with the flags of Texas and the U.S. flying above.

Nancy Ann recalls that, when she lobbied Warren to let her convert the former grocery store next to the restaurant's original cramped quar-ters into another dining room, he agreed only reluctantly, warning her that he didn't want to fluff it up and turn his place into some sort of ladies' tearoom. Not to worry. Clark's Outpost could never be described as ladylike. Its floors are uneven concrete; decor is a hodgepodge of pic-tures, letters, and newspaper clippings, souvenir baseball caps, bleached cattle skulls, and Gene Autry memorabilia. To keep the noise level low in the newer dining room, horse-blanket material is strung along the tin ceiling just above exposed heating ducts.

For years, eager entrepreneurs have tried to engineer a second loca-tion of Clark's in California, New York, or in the city limits of the

Dallas/Fort Worth metroplex, but Warren and Nancy Ann never gave such schemes a thought. "This place cannot be duplicated," Nancy Ann Clark says with unshakable conviction. "There can be only one Clark's Outpost, and that is in Tioga, Texas, horse country, USA. Where we are, north of Highway 380, it is a brand new world. We are friendly, we are relaxed, and most of all, we are an easy place to come for supper. When you sit down here, you can be certain you'll be getting something satisfying. Why, I've been to some restaurants in Dallas where the plate design is so beautiful and the portions so minute that you don't know what you're eating and you walk out wondering if you ate anything at all. We don't do plate design at Clark's. But we damn sure do beef."

Jalapeño Black-Eyed Peas

A favorite on Clark's menu since the early days, these luscious, zesty peas are good companions for any smoky meat. Serve them with white rice and you've got a kick-ass version of hoppin' john, the traditional southern New Year's Day good-luck dish. (Cavendar's seasoning is available in some markets, as well as from S-C Seasoning Co.: 870-741-2848.)

1 pound black-eyed peas, rinsed and drained.

2 beef bouillon cubes

2 garlic cloves, minced

3 fresh jalapeños, minced fine

1 cup diced white onion

2 bay leaves

2 tablespoons Cavendar's All-Purpose Greek seasoning, or 1 tablespoon oregano, 1 teaspoon crushed basil, 1 teaspoon crushed taragon

$1/2$ cup diced sweet red pepper

Salt, to taste

1. Soak peas in cold water 1 hour. Drain and transfer to large stockpot.

2. Place all remaining ingredients, except the red pepper and salt, in a large stockpot with about 12 cups of water. Bring to a boil. Simmer slowly until peas are tender, about 90 minutes, adding water if necessary. Add sweet red peppers for the last 15 minutes of cooking. Add salt to taste. Remove bay leaves.

Makes 10–12 side-dish servings.

Danish Inn Restaurant

ELK HORN, IOWA

*Y*ou could get off Route 80 in Elk Horn, Iowa, come to the Danish Inn Restaurant and eat a very nice hamburger or a BLT, or a plate of broasted chicken with French fries and cole slaw for lunch. Many folks who live around here treat the Danish Inn like an ordinary town café, which, in some ways, it is. They come for lunch or dinner and eat sandwiches or meat and potatoes, and don't give it a second thought. For those of us whizzing past on the interstate, however, the Danish Inn invites culinary adventuring.

Elk Horn is one of a handful of Danish-American communities where old-world traditions are not only a matter of pride but of regular celebration. (Elk Horn's Tivoli Fest is staged Memorial Day weekend.) Many of the citizens' ancestors established these towns throughout the heartland and as far west as Solvang, California, starting after the American Civil War. The area around Elk Horn was among the first and the largest of the settlements, especially favored by immigrants because its fertile fields reminded them of their home. The nearby town of Jacksonville was once known as Little Copenhagen and, to this day, the public schools of the area offer Danish language classes in the evening. Now, Elk Horn has a grand old grist mill, built in Norre Snede, Denmark, in 1848 and moved to America, piece by piece, in 1975, where visitors can buy stone-ground corn, wheat, and rye flours, as well as a large inventory of Danish imports.

Not far from the windmill, the Danish Inn Restaurant is the best place in town to sample a delectable heritage of old-world foods, including smorgasbords every Saturday night and Sunday at noon. The featured attraction on the buffet table is usually the consummate Iowan-Danish dish, roast pork—in this case stuffed with prunes and apples. There are sausages of every kind, *frikadeller* (pork and beef meatballs), and *fugles* ("birds," made of thin pieces of steak and bacon wrapped around a carrot, so named because they vaguely resemble something that can fly).

Among the sweet things to eat, which include puddings and cookies, one favorite Danish-American treat is *æblekage* (apple cake), a layered beauty customarily prepared in a glass bowl and served like trifle, with a spoon. Some recipes call for bread crumbs, others for crumbled cake. At the Danish Inn, they make their apple cake with macaroons—an inspired idea! If you don't have macaroons available, and want to use bread crumbs, add a tablespoon or two of sugar to the pan when you brown them in butter.

Æblekage (Apple Cake)

2 cups well-crumbled coconut or almond macaroons (the soft ones)

8 tablespoons butter

1 cup whipping cream

2 tablespoons sugar

2 cups peeled and coarsely chopped eating apples

$^1/_2$ cup raspberry jam, thinned a bit with water, if necessary

1. Sauté the crumbled macaroons in butter over low heat, tossing constantly, just long enough for them to absorb the butter. Remove from heat and continue to stir and toss to prevent sticking. Let cool.

2. Whip cream with sugar, until stiff.

3. In a $1^1/_2$- to 2-quart bowl, preferably glass or crystal, arrange alternating layers of macaroons, apple slivers, and whipped cream, making 2 layers of each. Swirl half the jam into each layer of whipped cream.

4. We like *æblekage* best served almost immediately, when the apples and macaroons are still crunchy. Use a spoon to dish it out like a motley pudding. It may be refrigerated and served later, at which time the flavors will have come together, and it will have become somewhat more cakelike.

Makes 6 servings.

Dodd's Townhouse

INDIANAPOLIS, INDIANA

*J*im and Betty Dodd started serving good food to the public at the Flag Pole Restaurant back in the 1940s. Thirteen years after that, they moved to the Townhouse, a one-hundred-and-fifty year-old former tavern in a residential neighborhood on the north side of Indianapolis. Since opening the Townhouse, the Dodds have developed a sterling reputation near and far for pan-fried chicken, thick beef steaks, and farm-fresh pies. Jim and Betty have since retired, and their son David took over. The last we tasted, the twenty-ounce T-bone was delicious, and the pie crusts as flaky as ever.

The Dodds skillet fry their steaks, so the steaks develop a wickedly savory crust to pocket all their juices. Slice into that T-bone, or the pound-and-a-half porterhouse, or even a smaller one-pound strip or "ladies' ribeye," and the natural juices spurt, then ooze, out onto plate. That's just fine, because it is a delight to push big hunks of chewy-skinned baked potato along the plate to mop up all the juices, or to dunk in a big shred of cinnamon bun for a combo of sweet and savory.

Nobody dresses fancy to dine at Dodd's but, somehow, everyone who bothers to come out to this place looks nice and acts polite. Service is fast but never brusque, and there is a feeling of well-worn familiarity about the whole experience. Most customers are regulars who have been dining with the Dodds for years, as well as a loyal clientele of out-of-towners (ourselves included), who wouldn't think of coming to the heart of Indiana without a visit to this wonderful old eatery. Here is the culinary equivalent of coming home.

No matter how much steak and potatoes or fried chicken you eat at Dodd's (and you will eat plenty), you must have dessert. You don't find pies like these too many places anymore: real blue-ribbon beauties, with feathery-light crusts and fillings rich with cream and butter, or with locally grown berries in the summer. You never know which pies will be available any particular day, but among the well-known specialties are chocolate, blueberry, and buttermilk.

Buttermilk pie, a heartland farm favorite, is a study in delicious simplicity. It has not too many ingredients, and it is easy to make. The only trick is to not overcook it or make the crust too brown. You want it as pale as sweet cream with a lemony zest. It will rise up in the oven as it cooks, then deflate as it cools. It is best served slightly warm, less than an hour out of the oven.

Buttermilk Pie

Dough for 1-crust 9-inch pie

1 cup sugar

3 tablespoons all-purpose flour

3 eggs, beaten

4 tablespoons butter, melted and cooled

1 cup buttermilk

$\frac{1}{2}$ teaspoon vanilla extract

2 tablespoons lemon juice

1 tablespoon grated lemon zest

$\frac{1}{2}$ teaspoon grated nutmeg

1. Preheat oven to 425°F.

2. Line pie pan with dough. Prick with fork and press a piece of aluminim foil snugly into the pan, covering the dough. Bake, 6 minutes. Remove foil. Bake, 4 minutes more, until edges of crust begin to turn pale brown. Remove from oven and cool. Leave oven on.

3. Mix together sugar and flour. Beat in eggs, then melted butter, buttermilk, vanilla extract, lemon juice, and zest.

4. Pour filling into cooled shell and bake, 10 minutes. Sprinkle top with nutmeg. Lower temperature to 350°F, and bake 30 minutes more, or until knife inserted in center comes out clean.

5. Remove from oven and cool. (Center will deflate as pie cools). Serve lukewarm. Refrigerate leftover pie.

Makes one 9-inch pie.

The Downing Café

*T*he town of Downing in the Chippewa Valley isn't on the way to anywhere, and has no branch of any national store or franchised restaurant. Among the handful of buildings on State Route 170 at County Road Q is Downing's Civic Hall, a sturdy red-brick edifice built in 1917. Up three steps to the portal of the front door, then down five steps into the basement, and you are in the Downing Café. It is a worn-smooth eatery with bare, laminate tables and a short counter facing the kitchen in the main dining room. Behind the counter, thick coffee mugs are arrayed by the dozens, ready for action. In the Northland, coffee is an *eau de vie*, consumed during every meal.

The semisubterranean café is the only restaurant Downing has ever had, a culinary town square for citizens, including the Glenwood High Walking Club, who trek the three miles from school every Thursday morning at six for pancakes or hot biscuits, and couples who come for spaghetti supper Wednesday night before the dance band starts to play polkas in the hall upstairs. Saturday is omelet day, when friends gather to eat eggs cooked in individual little skillets, along with heaps of hash browns. Sunday's morning business comes in shifts: after nine, when services conclude at Glenwood City's Catholic church, then after eleven, when the Lutherans of Boyceville and the Methodists of Downing have finished their worship.

The café has changed hands many times over the years, but its character and menu have remained constant. Current proprietor Delinda Karnes, who grew up in Downing, and worked as a waitress here during her teens, says that many of the people she used to wait on twenty years ago are still regulars today, as are their children. When she heard the café was for sale late in 1998, Delinda gave up a nine-to-five job in the Twin Cities to return to a life that is far more demanding of her time and energy, but one that she refers to as her homecoming. Now, she opens the kitchen every morning at four to make the pies, and stays through lunch and early afternoon, which is cookie-baking time. When we met her last spring, she was wearing a splint on her forearm from the repetitive stress of wielding heavy kitchenware. "The doctor told me not to do any cooking for a while," she laughs. "He might as well have said, 'Don't breathe!'"

Delinda is a strapping gal with an open face and a gentle smile who has made the old café her home. On the walls are country crafts for sale, including pot holders and wall plaques with wry or inspiring homilies: *A messy kitchen is a happy kitchen: Mine is delirious. God keeps His promises.* And one cartoon of silly-faced cows and sheep captioned, *Members of the Country Club.* Behind the cash register a sign announces, *If you are grouchy, irritable, or just plain mean, there will be a $10 charge for putting up with you.* In the entryway, at ground level, is a community bulletin board with signs advertising yearling horses for sale, an upcoming pancake supper, and a reward for a lost dog ("I have $75 and a lot of love tied up in

this dog. Last seen on Highway 64 West of Q. Reward to be paid to you, your church, or my church.") At the bottom of the stairs is a calendar with a county-by-county state map, posted courtesy of Dave's Body Shop.

"This building has been used for everything," Delinda says. "My parents told me the hall upstairs was a silent-movie theater; and I used to have a poster from a play put on there by a theater group—*Sally's Ship Has Come In*, I think it was called; it has been a high-school gym, a roller-skating rink, and a bowling alley. The front dining room of the restaurant used to be a barber shop; the back room started as a little library."

Few travelers ever accidentally find the café, and the only times Delinda ever advertised were to let locals know that she was planning to be closed: at Thanksgiving, Christmas, and Easter, and the Sunday after her parents' fiftieth wedding anniversary party (held in the hall upstairs), for which she and her siblings prepared a banquet of hot beef sandwiches. Hot beef is her family's favorite celebration feast, and as beloved a meal in the upper Midwest as pulled pork is in the Carolinas.

Hot beef is always on the Downing Café lunch menu—a jumble of dark chunks and shreds that are fall-apart tender, sopped with gravy. The beef is served as a sandwich or on a platter with twin globes of mashed potatoes veiled in gravy, and accompanied by a pile of soft green beans. One weekday, at eleven in the morning, we watched two hefty male tablemates in OshKosh B'Gosh overalls tackle their beef platters using an identical utensil technique: fork grasped in a firm-fist right hand, the way you'd grip a motorcycle's handlebar, and a slab of soft white bread folded in the left hand. The fork is slid under a heap of beef sideways, like a shovel; the bread is used to push as much meat as possible into balance on the tines. About every three bites, the leading edge of the bread has become so soaked with gravy that the fork is used to sever the moistened part and add it to the next forkload of beef.

Other than beef, the most popular meat for lunch is pork: baked chops every Tuesday and country-style (boneless) barbecued ribs on Thursday. Like many things that come from Delinda's kitchen, the sauce for the ribs starts as a commercial product, but winds up her own. In this case, she mixes two different barbecue sauces and seasons them until they have the right spicy-sweet flavor to complement the pork. For the Wednesday all-you-can-eat spaghetti special, she doctors up a chunky store-bought spaghetti sauce and serves it atop a plate of soft, pale noodles. While not a pasta of which Marcella Hazan is likely to approve, Delinda's unexotic but satisfying spaghetti makes us smile with thoughts of school cafeteria lunch at its nicest.

The signature of a true Wisconsin café is a large selection of pies, and there are several places in the state famous just because they are great pie stops. Back in the mid-1970s, we were oblivious to pie's power hereabouts, when we came across a tiny town café called the Norske Nook down in Osseo just off I-94, which we then declared to serve the best pie in the world, an assessment based primarily on its version of the local favorite, sour-cream raisin pie with a meringue top. At the time, the Nook was a lot like The Downing Café is today—a small gathering place for locals in a quiet little town; its cook and owner, Helen Myhre, made about a half-dozen pies every day. After our visit, Charles Kuralt came to pay homage on CBS, and Mrs. Myhre demonstrated pie making on David Letterman's show. She subsequently wrote a cookbook and sold the café, which has grown to become three gigantic family-style restaurants (in Osseo, Rice Lake, and Hayward), serving thousands of pies daily to throngs of hungry tourists. We don't expect the same fate to befall The Downing Café, safeguarded as it is by miles of slow country roads, but we will say this: Delinda Karnes' pies are forkworthy! The sour-cream raisin, powerfully sweet but with a faint sour-tang inflection, is thick and silky, loaded with soft raisins, perched upon a decent ready-made crust, and crowned with feathery meringue. Graham-cracker pie is twin ribbons of vanilla custard and white whipped topping, sandwiched between a spicy crust and a thick crown of sweetened crumbs.

"Cookies are nearly as popular as pies," Delinda tells us. "I have a hard time keeping up with chocolate-chip and sugar cookies; and a lot of people eat the oatmeal raisin for breakfast!"

The breakfast we recommend, other than the cornucopic farmer's omelet, is pancakes, accompanied by the succulent sausage patties Delinda gets from a supplier in LaCrosse. A normal order of pancakes consists of two enormous ones—about ten inches across and a good half-inch thick, so substantial that they seem less like ordinary flapjacks and more like two layers of a big, soft cake. Although it seems impossible that any nonfarmworker appetite could polish off two (you *can* order a short stack of just one), an all-you-can-eat deal is available for $4.25. It starts with three on a plate. In Delinda's recollection, only two customers have ever finished all three and asked for more.

Much as we enjoy eating at The Downing Café, its appeal is beyond the menu. Simply finding it, deep in farm country, is a joyous detour from eyesore interstates. County Road Q is a curving tour through woodlands and gentle hills, where dairy cattle graze, past hip-roof barns with hayloft doors and windows that look like the wide eyes and open mouths of flabbergasted faces. The farmhouses—aluminum modulars, Gothic wood-frames, and stone dwellings a century old—are well tended by their occupants, who are culturally disposed to be prolific in the art of lawn ornamentation. Displays include herds of plaster deer and cows, granny fannies, shiny runic balls on pedestals, and, quite often, a playfully lettered sign with the plural family name—the Bendtsons, the Albrechts, the Stoiks—along with the first names of the couple—Frank & Jan, Snort & Norma, Karla & Doyle—and sometimes even the names of all their children, in order of birth.

To walk through the café door is to enter the life of a town in a way that tourists seldom have an opportunity to do. For a first-timer, it can be disconcerting, given the fact that everybody knows everybody, and strangers are cause for at least a little curiosity. When we sit in the center room for our first lunch, virtually all the men and women who step to the nearby cash register to pay their tab note our presence, then say hello or offer a tip of the hat.

The next day, at lunchtime, we are greeted at the bottom of the stairs by veteran waitress Eddice, who grins ear to ear and announces, for all to hear, "You're back!" As we look around the dining room, we recognize about half the customers, sitting in the same places as they had been the day before. Seven days a week, the big tables are occupied for hours by an informal procession of folks who come to eat, pour their own coffee refills, and exchange news.

When we return Saturday morning, after not coming in for a couple of days, we are greeted by Delinda, who is seated at a table chatting with friends eating breakfast. She is conspicuously missing her wrist splint. "Heavens, what are you doing back here?" she asks with the gladness of a long-lost friend.

"We're hungry!" we respond.

"You're in the right place!" calls a woman in a Boyceville Fire Department jacket from a nearby table.

"And where's the splint the doctor said you should wear?" we ask Delinda.

"I can't write with it," she says, adding, "and I can hardly flip a pancake."

When Eddice brings our coffee pitcher, she too smiles that familiar smile that most of us reserve for friends or relatives we like. "Every time I see you, you're eating!" Eddice jokes.

"It's our job," we tell her. When we come across a place like the Downing Café, it's also our blessing.

Delinda's Graham Cracker Pie

This recipe for The Downing Café's most popular pie reminds us of the Minnesota farm wife we met a while back, who told us that one of her fondest taste memories was spooning into her first tub of Cool Whip after seeing it advertised on The Andy

Griffith Show. *Her family were dairy farmers; they had plenty of top-cream for their coffee, but for those extraspecial desserts that demanded a creamy element more stylish than everyday whipped cream, they reached for the new-fashioned whipped topping in the reusable plastic container. Although it is anathema to nature-worshipping foodies, Cool Whip is much preferred by many estimable pie makers in the heart of dairy country. Not only is it sturdier than whipped cream, it has a vivid sweetness and chemical complexity that plain sugar and whipped cream cannot equal. In fact, we tried substituting real whipped cream in this recipe, and it tasted puny compared to the crust and pudding; so, unless you are brave enough to be seen with Cool Whip in your shopping cart, don't even attempt making this genuine heartland pie.*

CRUST

2 cups graham-cracker crumbs $1/2$ cup sugar

$1/4$ cup melted butter or margarine

FILLING

2 egg yolks   2 cups milk

$1/2$ cup sugar   1 teaspoon vanilla

2 heaping tablespoons cornstarch   1 small tub Cool Whip

1. Coat a 9-inch glass pie plate with nonstick spray. Mix the graham-cracker crumbs, melted butter, and sugar, and pat into the pie plate, reserving about 2 tablespoons to sprinkle on top.

2. In a saucepan, over medium heat, whisk together the egg yolks, sugar, cornstarch, milk, and vanilla, stirring constantly until thickened. Remove from heat, cool slightly, and pour into the prepared crust.

3. Cool at room temperature or in the refrigerator ("I use my windowsill," Delinda advised). When cooled, gently spread the Cool Whip across the top and sprinkle on the reserved graham-cracker mix. Refrigerate. Serve cool.

Makes one 9-inch pie.

Dr. Mike's Ice Cream Shop

BETHEL, CONNECTICUT

*N*amed for the local dentist who devised the original recipes, and opened a back-alley ice cream shop in the 1970s, Dr. Mike's has been owned for more than twenty years now by Robert Allison. Robert is fanatical about ice cream; while other well-liked brands have expanded and franchised and become big corporations, Dr. Mike's has remained small. Here is one happy oasis of dairy goodness where the joys of making and eating ice cream still outweigh the business of selling and marketing it.

When we asked Robert Allison, who now ingenuously identifies himself as "Dr. Mike," why his ice cream is so good, he explained that cramped surroundings preclude mass production and mass storage. Despite great local success and national renown, he has purposely kept the facilities small, so as to never be tempted to make production more efficient. The only possible way to manufacture ice cream in his minuscule shop is daily, by hand, in small batches. Robert trucks down cream from a Massachusetts dairy farm, and makes his product with such maddening deliberation that you cannot count on any favorite flavor currently being in stock.

In fact, Dr. Mike's doesn't have a lot of flavors to offer. There are up to eight listed on the blackboard at any one time and, while the roster may change if cherry vanilla or mint chip gets eaten up, the repertoire isn't all that impressive. Neither is the restaurant itself. In fact, restaurant is much too big a word. Located down an alley behind the town's main street, this miniparlor has exactly three rickety tables on an open porch (no indoor seating at all), forcing most customers to eat leaning against their cars in the parking area. On a weekend afternoon, you'll wait forever to place your order at the tiny counter, where there is barely room for two employees. Such inconvenience does nothing to dissuade

Dr. Mike's diehards, for we are convinced that we have found the most delicious ice cream in the history of mankind.

Robert Allison's super-premium manna puts all factory-made brands to shame. His rich chocolate, always part of the flavor rotation, is a staggering foodstuff, its explosive Dutch cocoa taste carried in a custard as smooth as iced velvet. Chocolate Lace and cream, another standard flavor

here, is made of sweetened cream (but no vanilla flavoring) and big chunks of a Bethel-made brittle sugar candy sheathed in bittersweet chocolate. Fancy flavors, such as Heath Bar and Oreo, are made from a base of nothing but cream and Heath Bars or Oreos, without the eggs that are used by many ice-cream makers to thicken the custard. Even plain vanilla is a revelation: smooth and pure beyond description.

Dr. Mike's ice cream is never available prepacked, and it is awe-inspiring to watch Mr. Allison or one of the kids behind the counter fill a pint to order. Such a laborious process! A heavy trowel is used to retrieve a mass of your chosen ice cream from its tub and put it in the cardboard container. It is pressed deep, then more is fetched to mash on top. When the container is piled high with ice cream far above its rim, the pint-packer uses the trowel like a mallet, pounding to make the ice cream fit, even pushing it below the rim, so more can be laid on top. This continues until an impossibly huge amount of ice cream is compressed into the pint. The server takes the cardboard lid, expertly distends its top to form a cup-shaped hood, then eases it over the mounded ice cream, so that the band around the circumference winds up fitting like a belt you wore three sizes ago.

And, oh, what sundaes! A full-sized one totally fills a cardboard pint container once a shovelful of fresh whipped cream is piled on top. Among the toppings, take special note of the tart-sweet dark cherries, especially if chocolate-malt ice cream happens to be on the board that day. Mr. Allison also has perfected the art of making milk shakes. Never in twenty years have we once seen the blenders work efficiently. Once he puts all the ingredients in the tall silver beaker and puts it in the blender, he has to stand there poking at the ingredients and coaxing them to budge, so that the ice cream, milk, and flavors will mix. Without the prodding, the machine's wand simply doesn't have the torque to move ice cream so formidable.

Everything about this place bespeaks the single-minded passion of a man who has what he is quite certain is the best job on earth. "Who isn't happy when they're eating ice cream?" the boyishly slim Mr. Allison asked, as he swirled his tongue around a scoop of that morning's rich chocolate perched atop a cone. "I love it!" he told us with the unabashed glee of a ten-year-old boy. "I love it so much that I figure I need to make the best there is. If I didn't, I'd have to go someplace else whenever I wanted a cone."

Grape-Nuts Ice Cream

We've never figured out why Grape-Nuts became a staple in the Yankee kitchen and nowhere else in the U.S., where it is considered merely cereal. Many New England restaurants with a sense of local history offer Grape-Nuts pudding for dessert, and several of the best ice-cream parlors make Grape-Nuts ice cream, in which the crunchy cereal becomes a soft savory note in sweet vanilla-flavored cream.

If you have an ice-cream maker and a favorite recipe for vanilla, just add a cup of cereal to it. We use this rich formula.

6 egg yolks	1½ teaspoons vanilla extract
⅔ cup sugar	1 cup Grape-Nuts cereal
3 cups cream	

1. Beat the egg yolks with an electric mixer at high speed until pale and thick. Slowly mix in the sugar, continuing to beat.

2. Warm 2 cups cream in the top of a double boiler over hot water.

3. Gradually add about a cup of hot cream to the yolks, beating constantly. Then, gradually add the warmed yolks back to the top of the double boiler with the warm cream. Over moderate heat, cook and stir constantly using a rubber spatula to scrape the sides until the mixture is custard thick. Remove the top of the double boiler from over the hot water, and pour the mixture into a bowl to cool. Stir occasionally, and add the remaining cup of cream, vanilla, and cereal.

4. Freeze in an ice-cream maker according to manufacturer's directions.

Makes 2 pints.

The Enrico Biscotti Company

PITTSBURGH, PENNSYLVANIA

I was a small kid, the youngest of my family, and the older boys didn't particularly like me hanging around with them," says Larry Lagattuta. "So, I spent a lot of time with my mother and my aunts, in the kitchen."

God bless those nasty older boys! Today, the skills Larry learned at the side of the ladies of his family have made him the pride of Pittsburgh's Strip District, where his bakery, The Enrico Biscotti Company, is a beacon of great pastries and more. To watch him cut a loaf of biscotti for the cookies' second bake in the oven, or to flatten out the dough for a focaccia in a pan, or to sprinkle sugar and balsamic vinegar over strawberries for a balsamic-strawberry torte is to watch a natural at work. He never measures, never weighs, just does everything by touch and feel; it is a joy to watch him start with ordinary ingredients and produce spectacular things to eat.

Inside his tiny storefront bakery, the front counter is arrayed with about two-dozen jars full of extralarge, handcut biscotti in a variety of flavors, including classic anise-almond and black-pepper walnut, as well as white chocolate with macadamia nuts. Macaroons are a regular part of his repertoire, sometimes dipped in chocolate, and macaroon lovers everywhere agree that these are food of the gods. The inventory at Enrico can never be predicted exactly, for Larry makes what he feels like making but, every morning when he opens at six, regulars count on warm scones and, of course, biscotti.

Despite early education as a cook at his mother's knee, Larry spent the first part of his working life crunching numbers instead of kneading dough. "I was at Lucent Technologies for fifteen years," he says as he arranges discs of sausage from a nearby sausage maker atop a small pizza about to go into one of the back-room brick ovens. "I returned to baking for a little stress relief because I needed to get away from the tension of the corporate world. It was just a hobby. But then, suddenly, this little storefront on the Strip became available from a man I know and, before I knew it, I had the opportunity to open a bakery. I hardly had to think twice about leaving the business world. I knew what I had

to do. So, I cashed out and started to make biscotti. Then the space behind the bakery became available—it used to be a garage—and I took that, too, and was able to put in the bread ovens and a few tables, too. Now we've got a nice little café and people can come for coffee and lunch as well as pastries." To sit at Enrico Biscotti and sip espresso with a cookie on the side, is to know for sure that Larry Lagattuta is a man who has found his destiny.

Enrico Biscotti's Almond Macaroons

2 pounds almond paste (available at
  any good gourmet store)

12 ounces confectioners' sugar

12 ounces sugar

5 egg whites

32 ounces whole almonds

1. Preheat oven to 350°F. Line a few cookie sheets with parchment.

2. Combine almond paste, confectioners' sugar, and white sugar in a mixing bowl. Mix until it reaches a pealike consistency. Add egg whites, and mix until they are absorbed into the dough.

3. For each cookie, form about two tablespoons dough into a ball and place onto the parchment paper-covered pan. Place one whole almond on top of each cookie. Bake for 30 minutes, until the edges are brown.

4. Eat macaroons as soon as humanly possible.

Makes approximately 100 macaroons (they do freeze well).

The Farmer's Inn

*T*he Farmer's Inn of Havana, North Dakota, is the only restaurant for miles around. It is a place where neighbors come to hobnob and break bread together, where retired farmers hold court, where young men eat five-thousand-calorie breakfasts before a hard day's work, and where toddlers play (a box of toys is always on hand). One July fourth, a few years back, when the inn was open for breakfast until 11 AM, ninety-four meals were served—an amazing tally for a café in a dot-on-the-map town in the middle of nowhere, with a population of one hundred, not including dogs, cats, and livestock.

Havana used to be bigger. When Slim Miller opened the Havana Café in 1913, there were 450 residents of the thriving, grain-producing stop on the Great Northern rail line, just one mile north of the Dakota border. For decades, his restaurant served as an ad-hoc community club, where people could come not only to eat breakfast and the midday meal (known in this part of the country as *dinner*), but to exchange tidings over coffee. Slim sold the place in '48, after which several owners came and went. In the postwar years, many farms went from grain to row crops; agriculture modernized and small family farms grew scarcer. As time passed, Havana's population thinned, business at the restaurant dwindled, and the old café building began to crumble. Finally in 1984, the Havana Café closed, leaving the town without a restaurant.

It was only then that citizens realized how much the café had meant to them.

Jay Saunders, who runs the town gas station, put a pot of coffee in his office for visitors to share. American Legionnaires opened up their hall as an informal gathering place. However, neither of those well-meaning locales provided the kind of easy, come-and-go atmosphere of a small town café that is so conducive to a relaxed exchange of news and opinions.

Understanding that a restaurant in so remote a location had no chance of success if someone tried to operate it as a profit-making business, the Havana Community Club decided to reopen the café on their own. Men pitched in and fixed up the old building as best they could; wives volunteered to run the kitchen, agreeing to cook their specialties for neighbors, family, and friends one day a month. The Havana school had just closed (children now travel north to the bigger town of Forman for their education), so the refurbished eatery was able to get good appliances and equipment from the old school lunchroom. When The Farmer's Inn opened a few weeks before Christmas in 1984, a comical sign on the bulletin board reflected the true soul of a meeting place in the midst of a sparsely-peopled landscape: "Therapy Session 9 AM–noon and 1 PM–4 PM. No Charge."

About two-thirds of the town regularly came for breakfast and, some days, more than forty people showed up for dinner. In the bitter North Dakota winter, when temperatures drop far below zero, and farmers often finish chores early, tables were occupied throughout the day with pinochle players. And, from 6:00 AM on, the hot coffee never stopped

flowing. "If we charged fifty cents a cup, we'd be rich!" declared one volunteer cook last summer, as she watched a tall, thin gentleman in overalls help himself to what she estimated was his twelfth refill of the day.

Once the citizens of Havana realized their cooperative effort was going to work, they determined that the old café building was hopelessly dilapidated. They pooled their resources and built a new one, which opened in the winter of 1986 with a sign outside that says "Farmer's Inn

II." It is a utilitarian steel structure with a single spanking-clean carpeted dining room where wood-grained Formica tables are outfitted with hand-hewn wooden napkin holders in the shape of cows, pigs, tractors, and horses—all cut and painted by a local retired elevator operator (that's a *grain* elevator, by the way—the only structure around here more than two stories tall). A bulletin board includes a flyer for a polka band headlined by Jimmie Jensen, the Swinging Swede, and a manila folder tacked up with a note on it saying "Please Put Your Havana News in Folder." Items deposited find their way into the *Sargent County Teller,* which last July included such stories as: "July 1 Joe Barbknecht arrived and joined his family at the Walt Barbknecht farm." Our visit to the Farmer's Inn in the summer of 1996, when we wrote a story about it for *Gourmet* magazine, was front-page news, including a picture of us standing out front with the day's cooks: a retired wheat farmer and his wife and grandchildren.

Nowadays, instead of a different cook every day of the month, the rotation has been trimmed down to about a half-dozen cooks taking turns. Each is assigned a main course for every day on duty, but it is every person's job to plan the side dishes. The cooks we met made a point of distinguishing their cooking—farm cooking—from restaurant cooking. The latter, they said, is more deluxe, and uses ingredients they don't find in the grocery store and, worse, that their husbands wouldn't recognize. While not at all embarrassed to use canned soup for a casserole or cake mix for pineapple upside down cake, they also know how to make slow-risen, butter-horn rolls and old-fashioned knefla soup with hand-rolled dumplings. In the summer, they all make use of garden tomatoes and cucumbers in their salads and, when Harlan Clefsted returns from his winter home in Arizona, there will be pies made from the lemons he brings back from his lemon tree there. Mary Ann Fliehs is especially talented when it comes to pies—rhubarb, sour cream, lemon meringue, and coconut cream. Marie Underberg is delighted when the menu calls for roast turkey, because then she can make her big pumpkin cake for dessert.

"This is what I call a gravy-and-potato café," declares Harvey Peterson, whose wife Gloria is known for the raisin sauce she makes for baked ham when it's her turn to cook. Mr. Peterson, who has farmed the land for more than fifty years, is a café regular who, amazingly, drinks no coffee. One summer morning, at a table with his wife and some other cooks and his grandson Adam, who was about to turn two, he spoke of the days long, long ago, when Havana had four flourishing grocery

stores, two department stores, and a twenty-piece citizens' band for promenade concerts in the winter months. He recalled how empty the town seemed when the Havana Café closed. "Now, look at what we have," he said with a measure of pride, gesturing to a dining room crowded with Havanans, including oldsters bragging to each other about grand-kids' scholarships and batting averages, young families marshaling their members for a nearby tee-ball tournament, and working farmers engaged in an incredibly precise discussion about the spring wheat they raise—"the best, the highest protein"—versus white wheat, winter wheat, and soft red wheat.

"The Farmer's Inn holds our community together," Mr. Peterson concluded.

"It's like going to church on Sunday," one of the cooks added. "Except you don't have to be Lutheran to have your coffee here."

"Maybe we did save this café," another added thoughtfully. "But, the way I see it, this café saved us."

Mildred Brummond's Chocolate Beet Cake

1½ cups sugar

3 eggs

¼ teaspoon vanilla

1 cup vegetable oil, plus additional for greasing pan

1½ cups cooked and grated beets (about 1¼ pounds)

½ cup unsweetened cocoa powder (Hershey's preferred)

1¾ cups all-purpose flour, plus additional for flouring pan

1½ teaspoons baking soda

¼ teaspoon salt

½ cup water

1. Preheat the oven to 350°F. Grease and flour a 9-by-13-inch cake pan.

2. Combine sugar, eggs, vanilla, and oil. Beat well.

3. Add beets and cocoa. Beat again.

4. Sift flour, baking soda, and salt together, and add to the batter along with the water.

5. Pour batter into cake pan and bake 35 minutes.

Makes 8–10 servings.

Flo's

CAPE NEDDICK, MAINE

*H*ot dogs are the only thing on Flo's menu, so, when you enter this low-slung, six-seat diner and peer through the pass-through window into the kitchen, proprietor and chef Gail Stacey (Flo's daughter-in-law) will ask just one question, and it is not *What would you like to eat today?* She asks "How many?" These hot dogs are small, so we suggest you have a large number in mind. Three or four will sate a modest appetite. We've seen normal-sized men consume a dozen at lunch, allotting no more than two good bites per dog. Like the wieners, buns are steamed to order; and these gentle buns, fresh out of the heat box, have a fine, silky texture that is itself a vital component of the singular culinary experience of dining at Flo's.

Also crucial to the Flo's formula is the hot sauce—a devilishly dark sweet/hot relish of stewed onions, glistening with spice. A special at Flo's is a hot dog with this sauce, a sprinkle of celery salt, and a thin line of mayonnaise. This magic combination transforms a modest dog into something unspeakably luxurious. If, instead of mayo, you get mustard with the hot sauce, the kick of the sauce seems supercharged and every bite has a wicked bark.

For decades, the most important component of the dining experience in this legendary dog house was Flo herself, whose personality continued to infuse the joint long after she retired in the 1970s. When we met her in the late 1990s, Flo was 91 years old. She still lived on the premises and regularly ambled about the place, allowing herself one hot dog per week and making sure her customers behaved themselves. During her reign in the kitchen, Flo's became known as a place where diners were made to toe the line, or else. She called it as she saw it. "You're too fat for four hot dogs," she would say. "I'll give you two." Then there was the hapless trucker who stopped in late one lunch hour

for a cup of coffee. "What, you don't want any hot dogs?" Flo asked. The man said he had already eaten, up the road. "Then you go back up the road and get your coffee!" Flo ordered.

Flo Stacey passed away in June of 2000. Gail Stacey is still running the place as it's always been.

Not Flo's Hot Dog Relish

The onion hot sauce Flo devised for hot dogs is a top-secret recipe that we would not insult by trying to replicate at home. The truth is that the joy and flavors of the Flo's hot-dog–eating experience can be had only at Flo's. So, instead, we offer this snappy relish that we concoct for hot dogs when we are feeling more ambitious than just plopping on mustard. The recipe is eminently flexible. Adjust chili powder, sugar, and other ingredients, to taste.

1 cup diced Spanish onion

1 rib celery, diced

1 clove garlic, minced

1 cup diced red pepper

3 tablespoons sweet pickle relish

$1/2$ 6-ounce can tomato paste

$1/3$ cup cider vinegar

1 tablespoon dark soy sauce

1 tablespoon Worcestershire sauce

1 tablespoon chili powder

1 tablespoon sugar

1. Mix the onion, celery, and garlic in a microwaveproof bowl. Microwave on high, 1 minute. Stir. Microwave, 1 minute more.

2. Stir in all remaining ingredients. Chill overnight to allow flavors to harmonize.

Makes about 2 cups.

Frank & Mary's Tavern

PITTSBORO, INDIANA

*E*arly in the twentieth century, there was a car dealership on State Road 136 in Pittsboro that sold Overland cars. Overlands bit the dust, and the building became a hardware store, then a gas station, then a hatchery. About forty years ago, it became Frank & Mary's restaurant, one of the nicest places in the Midwest to eat catfish.

The history of the place, along with its décor, evocative of the Indy 500, add special flavor to the dining experience, because the meals served at Frank & Mary's long tables in the big old dining room are themselves a taste of tradition: midwestern Americana, from fried chicken or catfish or ribeye steaks to peppermint ice cream (a Hoosier favorite) for dessert. Waitresses are fast and friendly, and customers are Hendricks County regulars, as well as a few pilgrims from Indianapolis to the east, who drive out to Frank & Mary's because it has become a custom among families who relish downhome cuisine.

The food nearly everyone comes to eat is catfish. Since Frank & Mary's Tavern opened for business back in 1945, fish has been the specialty of the house. Originally it was codfish, cooked in an iron skillet and served as a sandwich, but, in the early fifties, the kitchen started serving catfish from Florida. Since then, catfish, also known as fiddlers, have been Frank & Mary's main claim to fame.

You can get whole fish or fileted tenderloins of catfish, nearly a pound's worth per order, encased in a crackling-crisp crust. Catfish epicures generally consider the whole fish better and more succulent, but, for novices, it can be some work to retrieve the meat from the bones. Filets are easy to eat, and although Frank & Mary's does not offer an all-you-can-eat supply like many Deep South catfish parlors, a dinner's worth won't leave you hungry. According to the extremely informative menu (where we learned the history of the business and the building, as well as of Frank and Mary Herring's family), excellent catfish is the kitchen's holy grail.

A word of warning is in order if you plan a trip to Pittsboro for catfish: Frank & Mary's gets mighty crowded on weekend evenings, and reservations are accepted only for parties of ten or more. Actually, crowded is the way we like it. There is a special flavor to a big, sweet catfish meal when you sit down to share it at a long table with a throng of fellow catfish connoisseurs.

Our recipe for catfish, inspired by Frank and Mary's, is for filets. If the place you buy fish sells tenderloined catfish, have them slice the filets about $1/4$-inch thick.

Hoosier Catfish Filets

$1^1/2$ pounds thin-fileted catfish	1 teaspoon ground black pepper
1–2 cups cold milk	$1/2$–1 teaspoon cayenne pepper, to taste
2 cups yellow cornmeal	
1 tablespoon salt	Vegetable oil, for deep frying

1. Rinse and thoroughly dry filets. Soak in milk, turning to make sure all filets are wetted.

2. Combine cornmeal, salt, and peppers in a wide pan.

3. Preheat vegetable oil in deep skillet or deep fryer to 375°F.

4. Working with a few filets at a time, move them from the milk into the cornmeal mixture. Roll them in the cornmeal until thoroughly covered, then set them individually on a piece of wax paper, not touching each other. Wait about five minutes for the corn meal to begin drying on the fish, then gingerly slide fish into hot oil. As the first batch fries, begin preparing the second. Cook each batch until golden brown, about 5–6 minutes. Drain on brown-paper bags.

Makes 4 servings.

Gordon's Coffee Shop

MILWAUKEE, WISCONSIN

*G*ordon's closed several years ago, but we will never forget this wonderful urban diner where Lenny Zuba showed us how to make great American-fried potatoes.

It took Lenny a while to warm to us; he pretended to be an irascible sort of character, and he displayed a prominent sign behind his counter that warned: NO SHIRT, NO SHOES, NO SOUP, NO SERVICE. We never tested Mr. Zuba's threat (we tend to wear shirts and shoes as we travel); in fact, we never saw anyone try to cross the tubby little maestro of the lunch counter, who identified himself, among other ways, with a plaque on his desk that said, "Leonard J. Zuba, Ph.D., Doctor of Fine Cuisine." Dr. Zuba's tenure at Gordon's began when he was fourteen years old, in 1936, when his uncle Al moved the hash house to its current location.

At breakfast, patrons used to occupy the counter on chrome-legged stools for hours, drinking coffee (brewed in a 1942-vintage machine) from thick mugs that looked like they had seen a million refills. Customers who came early and positioned themselves at one of the handful of tables called out their orders to Lenny at the grill, who went to work immediately, managing to carry on about a half-dozen conversations (sports, politics, local gossip) while also frying roast-beef hash, poaching eggs, buttering toast, and grilling bacon. This man was a hash-house pro.

His menu was pure diner fare, with special pride taken in the soups—all homemade, from scratch, selling for an unbelievable forty cents a cup in 1990. Chicken noodle, beef egg drop, vegetable: The repertoire was standard, except for those occasions when Lenny made Czarina soup, a Polish sweet-and-sour delicacy that takes three days to prepare.

Lunches were such things as hot roast beef with *real* mashed potatoes and gravy, bowls of chili, short ribs of beef with browned potatoes. No meal cost more than three dollars. In fact, the cash register at Gordon's was one of those oldfangled models that would not even log an amount more than three dollars! If two people feasted and ran up a tab of, say five dollars and seventy cents for burgers, French fries, and extra-heavy chocolate malts, Lenny had to ring up the total as two separate sales on his register: three dollars and two dollars and seventy cents.

Breakfast was always the highlight of the day at Gordon's, for that was when the air was perfumed with grilling beef hash and bacon, and there was plenty of round-the-room conversation among the regulars. The first time we found the place, talk focused on the city's impending sale of a local bridge, which Lenny contended he just might buy, so he could turn it into a toll bridge.

It was a delight to watch him create American-fried potatoes. An exacting process that he did by rote, the making of the spuds was a mesmerizing demonstration of hash-slinging skills. He sliced, he stirred, he buttered and oiled the potatoes without a second thought, all the while yammering on about how much toll he ought to charge when he bought his bridge. The highlight of the procedure—flipping the potatoes high in the air and catching them in their skillet—he did while hardly looking. We do not recommend such show-offy techniques when you try this recipe for American-fried potatoes—at least not until, like Lenny, you've been doing it for about half a century.

Lenny never bought his bridge, and Gordon's Coffee Shop has closed.

American Fried Potatoes

5 medium thin-skinned potatoes,
   scrubbed clean

3 tablespoons corn oil

Salt and pepper, to taste

3 tablespoons melted butter, or more,
   to taste

1. Boil unpeeled potatoes until cooked but still firm. Drain. Slice into $^1/_4$-inch discs.

2. Pour oil into a 6–7 inch cast-iron skillet. Turn heat to medium high and, when oil is very hot but not yet smoking, add the potatoes. (Stand back—fat will splatter.) Salt and pepper, to taste.

3. Let potatoes cook, 3–4 minutes, undisturbed, until undersides are dark brown.

4. Pour melted butter over them, then use a spatula to flip them. Cook, another 4 minutes, moving them around a bit with the spatula. If you like really buttery potatoes, add more butter as you flip. Not all the potatoes should be cooked equally. Proper American fries include some that are crunchy and dark brown, and others that are luscious and soft inside their charred and mottled skin.

Makes 4 servings.

The Grand Café

In Cochise County, south of Tombstone, Arizona, there is a border-town café with tremendous personality. The personality is mostly that of proprietor Vanesa Quintana, who learned the restaurant business at her mother's La Fiesta, a popular eatery in the town of Douglas for almost thirty years. During La Fiesta's reign, Vanessa and her mother were summoned to cater an affair at Ronald Reagan's White House, for which, she recalls, "We flew in everything, including our own avocados, to make sure it was authentic. The guests liked it. You know how I know? Because they went through ten gallons of hot sauce." She also remembers Arizona Senator DeConcini frequently coming into La Fiesta with a thermal chest so he could take chimichangas by the hundred back to Phoenix.

When her mother retired and La Fiesta closed in 1991, Vanessa opened The Grand Café in the town's old movie-theater building on its main street, across from the historic Gadsden Hotel. Here she presides over a menu of made-from-scratch Sonoran-American classics that include broad flour tortillas with melted cheese on top and limp grilled *cebollitas* (green onions) on the side, steamy green-corn tamales, and red or green chili beef, plus shrimp scampi, and an off-the-menu dark molé that attracts devoted fans from miles away. One other dish that puts this southern plateau destination on Arizona's good-food map is *capirotada*, the traditional Lenten-season bread pudding veined with sweet brown sugar and packed with apple chunks, banana slices, prunes, and coconut shreds.

"My husband Vicente is the chef," says Vanessa, a fashion-conscious siren who greeted customers one afternoon prancing on stiletto heels and poured into a tight black-leather skirt and button-popping blouse. "My husband is a great professional, and it is such a joy being married to a man who, when I come home from shopping, asks me what I would like to eat, then makes it for me." She leans close and confides with a wink, "He is also fifteen years younger than I am." Vicente, a strikingly handsome Mexico City native who tends the kitchen while Vanessa plays hostess in the dining room, listens, a bit abashed, as she boasts about his many talents, far beyond his culinary resume. He is a makeup artist, male model, occasional theatrical transvestite who does a sensational Madonna, and also a flamenco dancer. On occasion at the end of the day, he confesses, Vicente comes out of the kitchen to the small dance floor at the back of the restaurant to put on an impromptu show for diners and the staff.

If Vicente isn't dancing, it is quite possible some customers will be. The Grand Café is the sort of place that encourages you to punctuate the moment between your appetizer of *queso fundito* (a hot skillet full of melted cheese) and the *carne asada* (a broad chuck steak served with four-alarm pico de gallo) by heading back beneath the U.S. and Mexican flags and having a quick twirl with your partner. When the whim strikes her, Vanessa will add to the merriment by really dressing up, not as her beautiful self, but as Marilyn Monroe, a woman she deeply admires, and impersonates in local parades. Her respect for the movie star is a fact you cannot avoid in this restaurant, for the walls are plastered with images of Monroe, front to back. "I put up four posters of Marilyn when I opened," Vanessa says. "Then customers started bringing more and it snowballed. We now have hundreds of them. We even received a couple of nudes, but I had to put them upstairs. After all, The Grand Café is a family restaurant."

As of Spring 2001, The Grand Café was up for sale.

Capirotada

Butter, for greasing	$\frac{1}{2}$ cup raisins
1 cup brown sugar	$\frac{1}{2}$ cup chopped prunes
1 cup water	$\frac{1}{2}$ cup sliced Granny Smith apple
1 cinnamon stick	$\frac{1}{2}$ cup ripe but firm banana slices
2 ounces brandy (optional)	$\frac{1}{2}$ cup shredded coconut
12 slices white toast	1 cup shredded mild cheddar cheese
$\frac{1}{2}$ cup toasted pinon nuts	

1. Butter a 9-by-13-inch baking dish.

2. Preheat oven to 350°F.

3. In a heavy pot, stir together the brown sugar, water, and cinnamon stick and bring to a boil until it is syrup thick, about 15 minutes. Remove cinnamon stick. Stir in brandy, if desired.

4. Arrange six slices of toast in the prepared baking dish, tearing them to cover the bottom of the dish completely. Sprinkle on half of all remaining ingredients, then pour on half of the cinnamon syrup. Put the remaining six slices of toast on top and cover with all remaining ingredients.

5. Cover with foil and bake, 30 minutes. Remove foil and bake, another 10 minutes, or until top is brown and beginning to crisp. Serve warm.

Makes 10–12 servings.

Green Gables

*W*aitresses at the Green Gables don't carry much food. They wheel meals out from the kitchen on rolling carts. The carts, laden with food, glide among the tables of the big, bright dining room (with a glowing, lit-from-behind mural of Sioux City on one wall), where most of the customers at dinner are family groups, and nearly everyone seems to know everyone else. Green Gables is a friendly place; for strangers and travelers heading west, it provides a homey dining experience that will last a thousand miles.

On Saturday night, you might even have to wait for a table. This place is that popular among the locals; it has been a Sioux City favorite since it opened three-quarters of a century ago. The cuisine is folksy and mostly familiar, with a few quasi-ethnic oddities to make things interesting. Dinner begins with a basket of nice rolls, both dark and white, which arrive under a layer of plastic wrap—sanitized for our protection, no doubt. Then you choose from meat and potatoes, which includes barbecued ribs, an onion-smothered chopped beefsteak, and a specialty called Chicken in the Gables, which is half of a crusty-fried bird served surrounded by French fries, rolls, and slaw. They also serve nice filet of walleye pike, simply broiled with tartar sauce on the side.

Ann Landers once wrote that she believed Green Gables had the best fried chicken livers she ever ate—and it is even possible to get a bowl of matzoh ball soup!—but our favorite meal is Oriental chicken chow mein. This is a mountainous serving of stir-fried vegetables atop a bed of crisp noodles, topped with shreds of well-salted chicken and strips of fried egg. It is not like any chow mein we have eaten in a Chinese restaurant, but we like it: a real Chinese-American dish, with an emphasis on the American flavors and presentation. On the side, we drink lemonade—made with the juice of real lemons and sugar, decorated with a maraschino-cherry half, and served with a Flexi-straw.

To be honest, the thing about Green Gables that wins our hearts is the back of the menu. Here are listed the soda-fountain specialties: sundaes, sodas, and malts of every variety, including peppermint-ice cream hot fudge sundaes served with fudge sauce on the side, in a small, serve-yourself pitcher. The top-of-the-line treats get deluxe names, like The H-Bomb (an extraluscious soda), the Harem Share'm (a flaming extravaganza made with three kinds of ice cream and chocolate syrup), and the Goshawful Gooey (vanilla ice cream, orange sherbet, and marshmallow sauce). Give us a restaurant where they serve lemonade with a Flexi-straw and Goshawful Gooeys for dessert, and we are devotees for life.

The recipe for chow mein that follows is not exactly what you'll get in Sioux City. At Green Gables, they put the chicken on top of the chow mein. Our version is more like what you'll get in a Chinese-American restaurant, with the meat mixed into the rest of the dish. If you want to use about a pound of cooked shrimp or beef instead of chicken, or a combination thereof, feel free to substitute.

Siouxland Chow Mein

4 cups chicken broth	2 tablespoons dark molasses
2 cups diced celery (2 ribs)	1 tablespoon soy sauce
1 cup diced onion (1 large)	1 tablespoon butter
1 cup chopped cabbage (bok choy, if available)	2 eggs, beaten
	4 tablespoons cornstarch
2 tablespoons peanut oil	1 pound cooked, boned chicken torn into bite-sized shreds
1¹/₂ cups sliced fresh mushrooms	
1¹/₂ cups fresh bean sprouts	1 can chow mein noodles

1. In a saucepan, bring chicken broth to a simmer. Add celery, onions, and cabbage. Simmer, stirring occasionally, until celery is soft.

2. Heat peanut oil in large skillet or wok. Sauté mushrooms until they begin to soften. Add bean sprouts. Cook and stir until they are soft, too. Use a slotted spoon to add celery, onions, and cabbage to skillet. Add molasses and soy sauce. Stir and cook, adding enough broth to keep it moist and loose.

3. In a small pan over medium-high heat, melt butter; then cook eggs until firm, with minimal stirring. You want a thin egg pancake. Remove eggs from pan, season to taste, and slice into thin strips.

4. Dissolve cornstarch in the remaining chicken broth. Stir into vegetables in wok, and stir as mixture thickens. Add torn chicken.

5. To serve, put a layer of chow-mein noodles on each plate. Then heap on chicken and vegetables. Top with shreds of egg.

Makes 4–6 servings.

Hap Townes

everal years ago country singer Ray ("Ahab the Arab") Stevens
invited a New York friend to join him at one of his favorite Nashville
lunchrooms, a place called Hap Townes. The New Yorker was a
professional efficiency expert whose business was telling restaurateurs
how to be well organized. When he and Ray arrived at Hap Townes, a
one-room café in a remote neighborhood south of Music Row, a cluster
of people hovered outside the door waiting to get in. Inside, the line of
customers who hadn't yet eaten mingled with a line of those who had
eaten and were waiting to pay the cashier. The expert studied the con-
fusion and told Ray Stevens, "It will never work."

So much for experts, because Hap Townes was a Nashville institution
for more than seventy years, starting in 1921, when Hap began serving hot
lunch from an eight-seat pie wagon near the Nashville Fairgrounds. In
1946, Hap and his son, Little Hap, opened a small cookshop on Humphrey
Street near what was then the thriving May Hosiery Mill. Workers at the
mill needed a hearty meal that was fast and cheap, so Hap Townes—father
and son—set up a system to serve hot food, fast and cheap.

This is the way it worked: Customers entered the little building and
stepped up to a short counter where a member of the kitchen staff was
standing—stove to his right, pans of hot food in front of him, griddle in
back. He showed and told you what there was to eat that day. You made
your choice and he "dipped your plate," as they say in Tennessee. To dip
a plate is to pile it high with food straight from the stockpot and kettle.
You took your plate to a table and commenced eating; if you wanted seconds, you were free to return to the counter and get more. When finished, you'd stand up and tell the person at the cash register what you
ate and pay accordingly. It was fast—in and out in fifteen minutes, and
it was cheap—the most deluxe meal in the house cost $4.45 in 1995.

A midday meal of the type served at Hap Townes is known in the South *as meat-and-three*. The name says what it is: one meat from the day's selection of several choices and three vegetables from a daily list that is twelve or more items long. There are variations on the theme. You can choose to eat meat-and-two or even meat-and-one, and many customers come for meat-and-three *without* the meat, meaning an all-vegetable plate of three or four selections.

This distinctive style of dinner (*dinner* is the proper term for hot lunch hereabouts, supper being the late-day meal) is always served on heavy unbreakable plates with raised partitions that keep the pungent collard-green juices from running over into the sugary yam casserole, and is always accompanied by biscuits and/or cornbread and a tall glass of iced tea, followed by pie, pudding, or cobbler. The formula varies from place to place, and it may be listed on a printed menu merely as "plate lunch," but *meat-and-three* is the way true believers like to refer to it. That's because, like the places that serve it, the term *meat-and-three* is simple, direct, and on the level. In Nashville, it has a pulse-quickening effect, like the word *barbecue* in Memphis; it is a seductive incantation to lovers of paper-napkin cuisine, a phrase that holds the promise of glorious vittles served with utmost informality. One factor is constant about *meat-and-three,* and this is something that is true of virtually all the fine plate-lunch restaurants from Memphis to the Grand Strand: the *three* part of the equation represents southern vegetables in all their well-cooked, hog-jowl–flavored, vigorously seasoned, cheese-enriched, breadcrumb-gilded, margarine-sopped splendor.

Hap Townes shared with us one such recipe, for stewed tomatoes. It is a simple dish that is shockingly sweet. An excellent reminder that tomatoes are, in fact, fruits, not vegetables.

Hap Townes' restaurant continued in business until the mid-1990s, about ten years after Hap Jr.'s retirement. It is now closed.

Hap Townes' Stewed Tomatoes

1 28-ounce can whole tomatoes,
   including juice

8 slices white bread, well toasted

8 tablespoons butter

1 cup sugar

Place tomatoes and juice in a large saucepan. Tear toast into about 4 pieces per slice and add it to the tomatoes. Add butter and sugar. Simmer, uncovered, 20 minutes, stirring frequently. Serve warm.

Makes 6–8 servings.

Hopkins Boarding House

R ealtors value a property by comparing it to comparables but, in the spring of 2000, we came across an available rental so great that it has no comparables. It is a room at the Hopkins Boarding House in the North Hill historic district of Pensacola. The price is right—$125 per week—but what makes this address so extraordinary is that the rent includes meals. Spectacular meals. They are served the way Ma Hopkins used to do it—family style, at elbow-to-elbow communal tables, where platters of fried chicken, hot biscuits, sweet potato soufflé, and about a dozen other Dixie specialties fairly fly from hand to hand as everybody helps themselves to all they want. When the serving bowls get low, they are immediately replaced and, when you've finally had your fill, it's traditional to bus your dish and silverware to the kitchen window. Nonboarders then turn to the cash register and pay—$7 prix fixe—or have manager Betty Norris punch their meal ticket.

There are no current boarders at Hopkins Boarding House but, before Mrs. Hopkins died in 1986, her son Edward promised to uphold the sanctity of the culinary rituals she established since serving her first lunch to six customers in 1949. As always, the daily vegetable roster depends on what's in season. You can count on good biscuits and cornbread, and the entrée rotation never changes. Wednesday is chicken and dumplings, Thursday is roast beef, Saturday is ham. Tuesday, Friday, and Sunday are the gold-letter days for many regulars, for they are when fried chicken is the main course for lunch and dinner.

Ed Hopkins says that, before his mother bought the house, it had been an exclusive dining club, mostly for officers from Pensacola's Navy base. "Now *that* lady, she was strict!" he says. "She'd watch you eat and check your manners *before* she'd let you sit at her tables. Mother wasn't like that, but she had her way of doing things, and that was the right way, the only way. She grew up as the oldest of ten children, and it was her job to feed the family. She had only a sixth-grade education but, when it comes to running a kitchen and a dining room to feed great numbers of people well, I'd put her up against any C.E.O. She knew what she was doing. That is why I wouldn't think of changing anything."

Improper attire has always been forbidden at Mrs. Hopkins' tables, but the nature of a boarding-house meal precludes certain conventional table manners. For one thing, a boarding-house reach is completely appropriate;

in fact, it's rather impolite to always be bothering people at other areas of the table to ask them to please pass the cole slaw or apple salad, when it's just as easy for you to rise a bit from your chair and nab what you want, even if it means reaching far from where you're seated. A curious syncopated rhythm circles around a Hopkins Boarding House dinner table as diners rise and grab, sit and eat, then rise again for something else.

The strenuous business of reaching and grabbing is drastically reduced if you are lucky enough to get a place at the round table, with seats for ten, which has a large lazy susan in the center above the eating surface. All platters of food are placed on the lazy susan, which you simply spin to the left or to the right to get what you want. Here, a different sort of etiquette prevails. When you want to pile your plate with a spill of chicken and dumplings, you should lift the serving tray off the lazy Susan to do so, enabling others to be spinning it, while you are taking what you need. It is then your job to find an empty place on the lazy Susan to replace the chicken-and-dumpling platter and, when you do, you must put it there with the serving spoon facing inward. Spoons sticking out as the lazy Susan spins can be treacherous truncheons that knock over people's iced tea glasses.

The round table is especially in demand on fried-chicken days, for most platters of fried chicken contain a pulley bone (what Yankees call a *wishbone*), which experienced fried-chicken eaters want. It is coveted not for the luck it may bring, but for its meat. "Looky here!" says one happy customer as he snares the wishbone for himself. "Why there's more to eat on this big fella than on a whole breast." Not only more meat, we should add, but the most tender meat there is.

One other aspect of boarding-house etiquette atypical of ordinary meals is the speed at which people eat, despite the polite surroundings. Nobody dines at a leisurely pace. Even gracious southern ladies in frilly summer dresses and gentlemen in seersucker jackets sit down and dig in immediately and without hesitation, and continue eating and piling up their plate with more food until they are done. We suspect this revved-up boarding-house pace goes back to times when there was only a limited amount of food, and once a platter was emptied, it was gone. That's no longer the case, for empty Hopkins Boarding House platters are always replaced by full ones but, still, it's traditional to approach a meal here with the same enthusiasm a hungry dog attacks dinner.

Another etiquette lesson: You can talk with your mouth full. Speed eating seems to supercharge people's appetites for conversation, and it is rare indeed for anyone to sit through lunch or dinner in silence. Breakfast is another story, when many regulars sit buried in the morning paper while newcomers and strangers engage in awestruck odes to the wonderful tomato gravy that goes so well on grits and omelets, or to the most buttery, featherweight, flavorful pancakes in all the South.

In fact, much discussion at Hopkins Boarding House tables focuses on food. Betty and Clarke Wesson, who make a point of being first in the door at 11 AM at least three times a week so they can get a place at the round table, report that they recently came back from an ocean cruise on which the food was fabulous. "We ate the cuisine of a different country every day," Betty says as she slides four or five discs of crisp-fried squash onto her plate.

"And there was plenty of it," Clarke adds, holding out an empty biscuit basket for a waitress to take back to the kitchen and replace.

"Oh, it was very good," Betty assures us. "But it was nothing at all like this. This is my kind of food, food like grandma used to make."

Yes, indeed, there is something grandmotherly about the food . . . particularly if your grandmother was an accomplished African-American soul-food cook like Nellie Jones, who knows how to season the yellow squash overnight so that, when it is fried the next day, it transforms from a fairly bland vegetable into a disc radiant with earthy flavor and sheathed in a shattering crisp crust. Or like Cora Edwards, a Hopkins veteran of thirty-nine years and master chicken fryer who told us that her technique

is nothing special, but depends on using "the best oil you can buy . . . that, and the right seasonings." As to what, exactly, the right seasonings might be, all Cora could tell us was a little of this, a little of that, until the mix is just right.

And about that room allegedly for rent. Yes, it's still available, and the price is right. Ed Hopkins is just waiting for the perfect tenant—one who deserves to live above the best food in the South. The line forms to the right, ladies and gentlemen . . . and be sure to wear your best pressed clothes.

Mrs. Hopkins' Copper Pennies

Years ago we convinced Mrs. Hopkins to write down her recipe for cooked carrots. It required some interpretation, as she was not too specific about what size her "one sack carrots" was, or how long to cook anything, but we did manage to come up with this formula for a beguiling sweet-and-sour vegetable dish that has become a regular side dish at our home dinner table.

2 pounds carrots, peeled and cut into $^1/_4$-discs

1 medium green pepper, seeded and cut into sliver-thin rings

1 medium red onion, cut into sliver-thin rings

1 can tomato soup

$^1/_2$ cup vegetable oil

$^2/_3$ cup sugar

$^3/_4$ cup cider vinegar

1 teaspoon dry mustard

1 teaspoon Worcestershire sauce

1 teaspoon salt

$^1/_2$ teaspoon pepper

1. Boil carrots until cooked but still firm, about 12 minutes. Drain. Combine cooked carrots with sliced pepper and onion in a bowl.

2. Combine all remaining ingredients in a saucepan. Bring to simmer over medium heat. Remove from heat and pour over carrots, onions, and peppers. Stir well. Cover and refrigerate overnight. Serve cold.

Makes 8 servings.

Hudson's

COEUR D'ALENE, IDAHO

*P*ickle and onion?" the counter man will ask when you order a hamburger, a double hamburger, or a double cheeseburger at Hudson's, a counter-only diner that has been a Coeur d'Alene institution since 1907, when Harley Hudson opened a quick-eats lunch tent on the town's main drag.

Your garnish selection is called out to grill man Todd Hudson, Harley's great-grandson, who slices the raw onion to order, using his knife blade to hoist the thin, crisp disc from the cutting board to the bun bottom; then, deft as a Benihana chef, he cuts eight small circles from a pickle and arrays them in two neat rows atop the onion. When not wielding his knife, Todd hand-forms each burger as it is ordered, from a heap of lean ground beef piled in a gleaming silver pan adjacent to his griddle—all at warp speed. Customers enjoy the mesmerizing show from the sixteen seats at Hudson's long counter, as well as from the small standing area at the front of the restaurant, where new arrivals wait for vacant seats from midmorning through the afternoon.

Amazingly, there are no side dishes served at all: no French fries, no chips, no slaw, not a leaf of lettuce in the house. This is not to say the staff isn't attuned to the fine points of hamburgerology. When a man sits next to us and orders a glass of buttermilk to accompany his double cheeseburger, the counter man asks if he wants the beverage now, or three minutes from now, when his sandwich is assembled—thus ensuring the buttermilk will be served properly, ice cold.

Each patty is cooked until it develops a light crust from the griddle, but retains a high amount of juiciness inside. One in a bun makes a balanced sandwich. Two verge on overwhelming beefiness. Chef Hudson sprinkles on a dash of salt and, when the hamburger is presented, you have one more choice to make: Which condiment? Three squeeze bottles are deployed adjacent to each napkin dispenser along the counter. One is hot mustard, the other is normal ketchup, the third is Hudson's very spicy ketchup, a thin orange potion for which the recipe is a guarded secret. "All I can tell you is that there is no horseradish in it," the counterman reveals to an inquisitive customer.

Other than the fact that a glass case holds slices of pie for dessert, there is little more to say about Hudson's. In nine decades, it has honed a simple perfection so valued by townsfolk that, when a McDonald's opened down the street a few years ago, the franchise failed in a matter of months. Hudson's won the Coeur d'Alene burger war not by clever advertising or drastic price cuts, but by doing exactly what it has always done—executing a formula that brooks no revision whatsoever.

One day, at high noon, when an out-of-towner calls out above the lunchtime din to blithely ask, "Can you grill that onion for me?" all dialogue at the counter screeches to a halt. The question is so shocking that people actually stop chewing their food.

In the silence, Todd Hudson, back to the counter, doesn't even bother to turn his attention from the dozen patties sizzling on the steel grill before him. "No!" he calls out. And, with tradition reaffirmed, panhandle Huddy Burger devotees resume their lunch and conversation.

Hamburger 101

Two fundamental elements make an excellent hamburger: fresh-ground beef and an old grill. The meat should be 80–85 percent lean (leaner and the burger will be dry). Burgers are best formed by hand, but with as little handling as possible. A fistful of meat, 1/4 to 1/3 pound, should be formed into a circular patty no more than 1/2-inch thick. While it is possible to doll up the meat by infusing it with sauce, spices, minced garlic, and so on, a true American hamburger, as served at Hudson's, is beef, nothing more. We like ground chuck best.

The older and more used the surface on which the meat is cooked, the better. Years of cooking impart a seasoned quality to a grill or iron skillet that simply cannot be duplicated by a new one, especially not by a new one with a nonstick surface.

To cook a hamburger on a cast-iron skillet, it's best to make sure the skillet has a film of grease on it. We like to sauté a tablespoon or two of sweet onion in a bit of oil over medium heat, then scrape the onion to the side, thus leaving a slightly oniony slick on the cooking surface. Turn the heat to high, sprinkle a bit of salt on the pan, and slap on the beef patty. Salt the top. Give the patty 1 minute to cook, then carefully lift it from the pan and flip it. (Press the spatula hard against the cooking surface underneath the patty, in order to keep the hamburger from sticking as you lift it.) Never squish the patty down with the spatula, unless you like your hamburger juiceless. Once flipped, lightly salt the top again, if desired. Let the hamburger cook about 2 minutes. Flip again and cook, 1–3 minutes more, depending on the degree of doneness you desire.

Remove hamburgers from pan and place on buns. Top with onions, mustard, pickles, and so on.

John's New York System

PROVIDENCE, RHODE ISLAND

here the Elite Meet to Eat augurs the sign outside John's New York System restaurant across from the old Cranston Armory in Providence, Rhode Island. Despite the motto, it is unlikely you will encounter many highborn aristocrats hobnobbing at the seven low counter stools in this short-order café in a less-than-glamorous part of Providence. You can be sure of rubbing elbows with the most discriminating urban hot-dog connoisseurs and, if you are lucky, you'll meet Viola Degaitas, seventy-something widow of John and mother of Henry, who now runs the place. Viola is the maker of the rice pudding and split-pea soup, and keeper of the formula for John's chili sauce. With the lush accent of a woman more comfortable speaking Greek than English, she smiles a beatific smile and shows off a big tureen, full of raw onions, which she cuts every morning to garnish the hot dogs, and demonstrates exactly how to line up a dozen hot-dog-filled buns for dressing with condiments and chili sauce—"back to back, belly to belly," she says.

When we ask her about the term *wienies up the arm*, an old Rhode Island hot-dog maker's trick of lining up the dozen from wrist to shoulder to be dressed, Mrs. Degaitas disapproves. Yes, she confesses, her husband used to do it that way. But she is proud to say that her son Henry lines them up on a plate, not along his arm. Thus he never produces what has long been known among Ocean State café society as a *pit dog*, the wienie no one wants.

Henry is amazing to watch behind the counter, dressing dogs at high speed, working the griddle with his spatula, taking to-go orders on his headset telephone, and sliding unbreakable plates of food along the counter to their intended. "My father called this 'New York System' because, in the 1940s, 'New York' meant stylish," Henry says. "But, you know something funny? They never had wienies like this in New York."

He is absolutely right. Rhode Island's tiny, steamed-pink wienies, topped with zesty chili sauce, are as different as a hot dog can be from a crisp-skinned, New York-style kosher frankfurter.

Rhode Island's distinctive New York System hot dog, as served to perfection at John's, is nestled in an untoasted bun, topped with yellow mustard, chopped raw onions, and a dark sauce of finely ground beef. It's the sauce that makes the dog—spicy but not hot, made without tomatoes, yet vaguely sweet, reminiscent of the kaleidoscopic flavors that give Greek-ancestored Cincinnati five-way chili its soul.

When we ask Henry what exactly is in it, he gladly begins to enumerate: "Allspice, chili powder . . ." But, before he can get further, Viola Degaitas comes along and gives him a firm whack on the shoulder.

"Never tell how you make your sauce!" mother says. "When you have sons, they can know."

New York System Chili Sauce à la John's

Chili-sauce recipes for hot dogs are sacred, guarded like the formula for Coca-Cola. However, after careful study and not a little prying, we came up with the following blueprint for producing a chili sauce in the style of New York System restaurants that is eminently suited to franks of any pedigree, all beef or porky.

1/2 cup finely chopped onion	1 teaspoon allspice
1 clove garlic, minced	1/2 teaspoon nutmeg
2 tablespoons vegetable oil	1/2 teaspoon celery salt
1 pound lean ground chuck	1/4 teaspoon ground ginger
1/2 cup beef broth	1 teaspoon ground cumin
2 teaspoons chili powder	1 tablespoon soy sauce
1/2 teaspoon freshly ground black pepper	

1. Sauté onion and garlic in vegetable oil until soft. Add ground chuck and cook until it is browned, stirring constantly with a fork or spatula to keep it broken up. Drain excess oil. Add the beef broth seasonings and soy sauce. Simmer, 10 minutes, or until most of the liquid is absorbed.

2. Put this mixture in a food processor and pulse, 4–6 times, to finely grind the meat.

3. The sauce goes *on top* of mustard and raw onions. It is zesty, so use it sparingly.

Makes enough to dress 8–10 modest-sized hot dogs.

Johnnie's Grill

EL RENO, OKLAHOMA

As culinary genealogists, we hit a wall in El Reno, Oklahoma. After a few days eating our way around town, we left more confused than when we arrived concerning the family tree of El Reno's renowned onion-fried burger. Like many Western legends, the truth varies, depending on who's telling the tale. Some locals say it was invented by a couple of train men in the early 1900s, who yearned to start a business and settle down in this Route 66 community just west of Oklahoma City. Others attribute its origin to Ross Davis, who opened a place called The Hamburger Inn some time in the 1920s. However the onion-fried burger started, it is now a town passion, and there are few citizens whose lives aren't perfumed in some way by this distinctive variation on the all-American meal-on-a-bun.

There are currently four restaurants in El Reno that are known for their onion-fried burgers—more than a dozen have come and gone since the 1920s—but three of them do not list "onion-fried burger" on the menu. In this town, when you order a hamburger, you will get an onion-fried burger, unless you specifically instruct the cook to leave the onions out.

There was a time when onion-fried burgers were far better known to travelers than they are today. Before I-40 relieved automobilists of the necessity (and the joys) of driving along the main streets of southwestern towns and cities, Route 66 was the major artery between the Osage Frontier and panhandle of Texas, with El Reno smack in the middle, at the crossroads of Highway 81. From the 1930s, well into the 1950s, wayfarers along the Mother Road couldn't help but know about El Reno's specialty as they drove into town: Its prairie air is always laced with the perfume of cooking onions.

As we devoured a brace of onion-fried burgers in a counter-only café called Robert's, we asked proprietor Edward Graham to fill us in on burger history. By its looks, we assumed that this place must be the town's original burger place, for it is a classic old diner and is, in fact, El Reno's oldest extant hamburger shop, going back to 1926. "Robert is gone," Mr. Graham told us. "He now owns Jobe's." (Jobe's is a drive-in on the outskirts of town that still features car berths with working Ordermatic menus that have built-in walkie-talkies for placing orders. Double-meat burgers and triple-decker burgers are delivered to your window by carhops.) "But Robert was not the one who started this place," Graham continued. "I believe it was built by two brothers who called it Bob's White Rock. They planned to open White Rocks all over the West." Graham was quite certain that the brothers were not the inventors of the onion-fried burger, just entrepreneurs who wanted to promulgate it.

Steve Gallaway, who owns a 560-square-foot burger shop called Johnnie's Grill, having bought it in 1995 from Otis Bruce (who now works as Johnnie's grill man), himself bought it in 1967 from founder W.J. "Johnnie" Siler, gave us what he claimed was the definitive story—about a pair of peripatetic railroad men conceiving the onion-fried burger nearly a hundred years ago.

The longer we spent in El Reno, the more confused we became about the intricate relationships of the town's various hamburger chefs, all of whom seem to like and admire each other (and many of whom have worked for each other), despite the fact that they are competitors. Finally, we felt we had a good shot at determining onion-fried burger provenance when we walked into Sid's, a block east of Robert's, where proprietor Marty Hall (who learned the business working at Johnnie's) has filled his place with archival photographs of old El Reno. Using eleven gallons of clear epoxy to seal some 450 images onto the top of the counter and the tops of tables, he arranged things in chronological order, starting at the far left of the restaurant. Mr. Hall's visual history long predates the onion burger and includes pictures of Chief Black Kettle, later killed west of town by a young George A. Custer in the Washita Massacre, and Cado Jake, who ran a ferry across the South Canadian River. Hall pointed to a photograph of his greatgrandfather, a sure-enough cowboy in Stetson hat and chaps, on a horse with rope and saddle, who homesteaded west of town in the early 1900s. "Did you know that El Reno was once larger than Oklahoma City?" he asked. "This was the western border of civilization. Beyond here was Indian territory."

Despite his fondness for history, Mr. Hall couldn't tell us much about the onion-fried burger's origins. He did explain that his restaurant is named Sid's after his dad, whose dream was to open a hamburger place, but who passed away before he and his son could do it together. As we left Sid's, still wondering when and where the unique burger began, Mr. Hall did provide us with a nice summary of how the onion-fried burger fits into the small town's allure. "A hamburger, good people, and Route 66: You won't get more American than El Reno."

The next morning, while at Johnnie's counter eating Arkansas sandwiches (that's a pair of pancakes layered with a pair of eggs), we finally did find what seems to be an authoritative description of the onion-fried burger's beginnings. Proprietor Steve Galloway and former proprietor (now grill man) Otis Bruce introduced us to Bob Johnson, who, as usual, had come for breakfast. Mr. Johnson said with certainty that it was his father, along with a man named Ross Davis, who opened El Reno's first onion-fried burger restaurant, The Hamburger Inn, in the 1920s. About ten years later, Mr. Johnson's uncle, Darrell Hurst, bought it; then, in World War II it was taken over by a guy remembered only as Hindy. In the early 1950s, Ross Davis bought it back from Hindy. "That's when I lost track," Mr. Johnson confessed. "I moved to Alaska in 1957 and, when I returned in '75, Ross had opened Ross's Drive-In (although The Hamburger Inn was still operating, under other management)."

The twists of hamburger history sent our heads reeling, but we perfectly understood Mr. Johnson's heart-rending expression of what it was like to spend eighteen years in Alaska, where onion-fried burgers do not exist. "I tried to make them out of moose and caribou as well as beef, but it was never right because I only had a skillet, not a thick, seasoned grill. To make a good onion-fried burger, the grill has to be *well*-seasoned . . . and there are a lot of well-seasoned grills in El Reno."

How to Make an El Reno-Style Onion-Fried Burger

¹/₄ pound ground beef, about 80% lean   ¹/₃ cup slices paper-thin yellow onion

1. Form the beef into a sphere and slap it onto a hot, lightly oiled griddle or into a hot, well-seasoned, cast-iron skillet.

2. Place the onions atop the round of beef. Use a spatula to flatten the onions into the beef as you flatten the beef into a circular patty. Press down 3 or 4 times to create a broad patty, changing the angle of attack each time you press, and mashing the onions deep into the top of the soft, raw meat.

3. Once the underside is cooked to your liking, flip the hamburger so that all the ribbons of onion are now on the underside. Give it enough time for the onions to begin to caramelize, then carefully use the spatula to scoop up the burger and fried onions and place this patty on a bun, *onion side up*. Lettuce, tomato, mustard, and pickles are all optional.

Makes 1 onion-fried burger.

Katz's

Katz's has been part of Houston Street on New York's Lower East Side since 1888. A big painted sign outside offers the enigmatic slogan, *"Katz's—That's All!"* of which we only recently learned the meaning. Many years ago, when the proprietor decided he needed a new sign, the sign painter he hired asked him what he wanted the sign to say. The proprietor replied with the obvious: "Katz's."

"Nothing else?" the painter asked, yearning to have a little more to work with.

Slightly exasperated, the owner answered, "Katz's—that's all." And that is what he got.

Inside, this relic of bygone New York operates like an old-time urban deli: You get a ticket when you enter and, as you order food at the counter, the ticket is marked accordingly. Pay on your way out.

It is a cavernous eating hall with lined-up tables, the air filled with the noise of shouted orders and clattering carving knives and the aroma of the odoriferous garlicky salamis hanging along the wall. Pictures of happy celebrity customers ranging from comics Jerry Lewis and Henny Youngman to a former police commissioner are everywhere.

For a greenhorn, merely getting food can be an intimidating ordeal. Ordinary table service by waiters is available, and quite easy, but that is the coward's way. To earn your stripes at Katz's, you must personally engage wits with a flinty-eyed counter man. Here's how: Take your ticket to the nose-high counter and make eye contact with one of the white-aproned carvers who is busy slicing meats and making sandwiches behind the glass. Once you've gotten his attention, be quick, and tell him what you want: pastrami on rye or on a club roll, or corned beef or brisket. Not one of these guys would win a Mr. Congeniality contest, but consider yourself blessed if your counterman happens to be Krinsky, a professional sourpuss/straight-man comic who has been slicing meats at the Katz's counter since the days of the Pharaohs. To crank Krinsky up to full speed, ask for white bread (there is none) or a little mayonnaise for your sandwich (they do have it, but hidden away), and he will go into a kabukilike routine of dramatic sighs and eye-rolling that make it clear he can barely live through another moment of your benightedness.

"Where are you from?!" Krinsky barks when, just to yank his chain, we ask him to explain the difference between corned beef and pastrami. (Pastrami is beef that is cured in brine, corned beef that is, then spiced and smoked.) Instead of answering with words, which would pain him too greatly and take longer than the proverbial New York minute, he takes his carving knife and in about three-quarters of a second, lops off a slice of each, and forks it over the counter for us to taste.

When the meat is cut (all by hand, of course) and the sandwich assembled, it is plated with a pickle. The counterman then uses a grease pencil to mark its cost on the ticket you received on the way in. You then carry the plate and ticket to the far end of the counter for French fries or a Dr. Brown's Cel-Ray soda, or to the near end for an egg cream, where the ticket is marked up accordingly by the staff. Then carry your food to a table and feast.

Even if you don't enjoy the attitude (we find it fun, as if Don Rickles had become a restaurant), all is forgiven when you heft a Katz's pastrami sandwich: three-quarters of a pound of meat that has been expertly severed into pieces so chunky that the word *slice* seems too lightweight to describe them. Each brick-red, glistening, moist hunk is rimmed black, redolent of garlic, smoke, and pickling spices, as savory as food can be. You can pay a dollar extra to have it cut extra-lean, but it is hard to imagine these taut, pink slices any leaner than they are.

"We go through five thousand pounds of pastrami every week," says owner Alan Dell, who happens to stroll by our table and stop when he hears us groaning with delight over his delicious sandwiches. Apparently, our rapture is so audible that he compares us to the pros and says, "What, you're not sitting at the *When Harry Met Sally* table?" He points to the one at which actress Meg Ryan did her show-stopping fake-orgasm scene while eating Katz's food, which prompted the comic line, "I'll have what she's having." "You know, I counted: Billy Crystal ate six pastrami sandwiches when they filmed that," Mr. Dell reports. "And between sandwiches, he was at the counter eating hot dogs." (Although we missed sitting at Meg and Billy's table, we did manage to secure seats at the one where a hand-lettered sign advises: *You are sitting at the table where Vice Pres. Gore and the Prime Minister of Russia had their deli summit lunch.*)

Mr. Dell, wearing a Katz's souvenir shirt that implores "Send a Salami to Your Boy in the Army," engages us in a Socratic dialogue about pastrami's roots. "Who invented it?" he asks.

"Romanians," we say—the traditional history-book answer.

"And why?"

"Pickling and smoking are ways of preserving meat without refrigeration." Again, we give the standard explanation.

"Aha!" he says, raising a forefinger in the air. "Who else preserved meat that way? Who else didn't have refrigerators?"

We are stumped.

"American Indians!" he says. "That's the new twist. They invented pastrami, long before Jews came to America." As we marvel at the theory, Mr. Dell adds in a low voice, "Of course, they had no rye bread or pickle." He then seamlessly segues into a monologue about all the TV shows and movies that have come to Katz's because it offers such a colorful slice of city life. Before strolling away to shmooze with other customers, he offers a grand finale to his recitation: "If it's New York you want, Katz's is the spot!"

Pastrami and Eggs

One of the great things to do with pastrami, other than put it in a sandwich, is to use it in a deli-style (unfolded) omelet. Salami, tongue, corned beef, or bologna can all be used in the same way but, if you've got good pastrami, it's the best. This recipe comes from Alan Dell of Katz's. In a kosher kitchen, chicken fat would be used, but Katz's, being kosher style rather than orthodox, uses regular cooking oil. We like the taste of butter . . . although it might give Krinsky a fit.

2 tablespoons butter	3 eggs, beaten
3–4 large slices pastrami (about $\frac{1}{4}$ pound)	Rye toast and/or hash browns, for serving

Heat the butter in an omelet pan over medium-high heat, then throw in the pastrami and fry it on both sides for a few moments, until the meat is warmed and the fat begins to look translucent. Pour in the eggs. As they cook, use a wooden spatula to pull the cooked parts towards the center, allowing uncooked egg to run onto the pan. When the bottom is lightly brown and the top almost set, flip the omelet, and cook it a moment longer.

Serve immediately, with rye toast and/or hash-brown potatoes.

Makes 1 omelet.

Kitchen Little

*F*lo Klewin, whose father supervised family clambakes and whose mother ran the Pilot House restaurant in Stonington Village on Connecticut's easternmost shore, is a woman who knows chowder. At Kitchen Little, her restaurant in Mystic, she serves a kind of chowder never found down east, to the west, or anywhere else, for that matter. It is a seafood soup unique to eastern Connecticut and Rhode Island—clear-broth clam chowder, sold by the bowl or in a crockery coffee mug.

Made with no cream or milk, and no vegetables other than potatoes and onions, clear broth chowder is a potent elixir that radiates marine fragrance like a summer breeze across a white-sand beach. It is served in small portions to whet the appetite before a whole lobster feast or a clambake, or a wide bowl of it with a stack of crackers on the side makes a warming winter meal.

"It is the only chowder I knew growing up in Mystic," Flo explains when we chat with her in the galley-sized kitchen of the diminutive café between the highway and the historic seaport where tall ships are berthed. Flo's chowder is some of the best of its kind. Crowded with large pieces of tender pink clam, as well as soft hunks of red-skinned potato, dotted with fresh basil, this is an exhilarating soup with uncomplicated oceanside character.

Other than chowder, the one essential seafood to eat at Kitchen Little is scallops, listed on the menu as "Stonington scallops." Savvy local mollusk fanciers know that *Stonington* refers to the home berth of the scalloper *Patty Jo*, which Bill Bomster and his crew use to harvest sea scallops south of Georges Bank off the coast of Cape Cod. Bomster family scallops are a local legend—prized by a handful of top-flight seafood restaurants and fishmongers for the fact that they are shucked and fresh frozen within two hours of coming on the boat. At Kitchen

Little, Flo encases Bomster scallops with a light batter and quickly fries them, resulting in frail-crusted, pillowy nuggets that are dense, sweet, and pure.

Most travelers who know and love Kitchen Little are probably unaware of the chowder and scallops, good as they are. What has put this little gem of a roadside restaurant on the good-eats map is breakfast. In the morning, every one of its twenty-three seats (including five stools at the short counter) is constantly occupied by people who come for omelets and pancakes.

Waiting is such a fundamental part of the Kitchen Little experience that one man wrote a poem about it, now inscribed in calligraphic handwriting and posted in the tiny vestibule.

KITCHEN LITTLE
This place is small but it stands tall, stands out above the rest;
With room for all, may have to wait, but the food is the very best.
The smiles you see, maybe people you meet, will make it worth your time;
Sometimes to reach the best places in life, we have to stand in line.

> Thank you,
> Bill H

If you are a party of two, when your name comes up a waitress will escort you into the dining room and point you to the open deuce. For singles, there is the short counter or, as a sign advises, "Make a new friend by joining a table." The place is absolutely packed—it is a mere four hundred square feet, including the kitchen—and the seats are so close together that at the counter, and even at the eight small, glass-topped tables, you always run the risk of reaching down and picking up your neighbor's coffee mug instead of your own. It is virtually impossible to carry on a really private conversation.

A galley kitchen facing the counter provides the sounds of bacon sizzling and eggs being scrambled as an appropriate background beat for gregarious morning chatter that fills the café air. One summer morning, we are mesmerized by a current-events colloquy carried on through the kitchen's pass-through window between Joyce Fitts, the weekday cook (and regionally successful dragster driver on weekends), and a couple of fisherman types perched on counter stools nursing coffee. The customers both agree that one of Connecticut's United States senators "doesn't have both oars in the water"; alas, the conversation drifts into Kennedy family gossip before we can discern which senator they are talking about, and precisely what his problem is. At a table next to ours, two women waiting for their breakfasts to arrive each hold sections of the morning newspaper in front of their faces, commenting to each other on the advice of Dear Abby and the poor performance of their high school sports teams.

"Oh, you are a great cook!" calls a patron fifteen feet clear across the dining room toward Joyce in the kitchen.

Joyce hollers out her thanks while slinging eggs onto the griddle.

"You want to come to Florida?" the enthusiastic customer beseeches. "We need you there. I've got nothing to eat for breakfast where I live!"

"Meep-meep!" honks waitress Annie Vos like the cartoon Roadrunner in an attempt to pull the ladies' attention from their paper. She has two plates piled with tall, sunny-yellow omelets, one filled with glistening green leaves of spinach, mushrooms, and cheese, the other made with chunks of rugged Italian sausage. (The ladies' table is so close to ours that it is tempting to steal a taste straight off their plates.) "I hate to interrupt you," Annie says, "But you'd better eat while it's hot."

Once the omelets are set down, Annie spins to address us. Somehow, the staff have perfected the technique of negotiating the interstices between tables, and they seem to be everywhere, all the time. "Ready to order?" she asks.

"We need a minute," we reply.

"You got a minute!"

As the clock ticks, Annie twirls toward another table and fields a query about the population of the beautiful flowerbeds that ring the little restaurant, which are her responsibility. (And it is Annie's mother who makes the supersweet German chocolate cake that is frequently offered as a lunch dessert special.)

Our sixty seconds up, Annie turns to us.

"We'll have pancakes," we say.

"You want the pancakes, or you want the C?" Annie inquires, referring to the third daily special, listed on the chalkboard after (A) fresh asparagus, carrots, and Swiss cheese omelet, and (B) grilled hot sausage, home fries, and jalepeño peppers topped with scrambled eggs and jack cheese. "You order pancakes, that's all you get. You want warm strawberry sauce, you better say C."

C it is.

The pancakes are big and tender with a buttermilk tang, and the sauce is tart, but it's the egg dishes most people come to eat. Flo Klewin tells us she goes through ten thousand dozen eggs per year. In particular, we recommend the S'medley, a contraction of Sue's Medley, to honor Susan Davis, the woman who originally transformed the little building

that had once been a private home, then a rug shop, then a greasy spoon, into Kitchen Little, back in the late 1970s. (Flo started as her waitress, and took over the business when Sue left in the mid-1980s.) The S'medley is a great hot heap of fluffy scrambled eggs with cheese melting on top, blanketing crunchy home fried potatoes, sausage, mushrooms, and onions. Another of Kitchen Little's scrambled egg medleys is the Portuguese Fisherman, made with linguiça and chorizo sausage Flo gets from a butcher in Fall River, Massachusetts—also the source of Portuguese sweet bread which is frequently made into a weekend special of sweet-bread French toast.

Waitresses patrol the tiny dining room with a pot of coffee in each hand—regular and decaf—topping off your cup nearly every time you take a sip. For most of us, the coffee is served in Kitchen Little souvenir mugs that are inscribed *Is There Life Before Coffee?* Frequent patrons, on the other hand, keep their own cups hanging on hooks just above the counter—about sixty of them altogether, a miscellaneous mug collection of silly cartoons, fine-art reproductions, souvenirs, and earthenware. When a member of the kitchen staff catches us admiring this homey touch, she bemoans the collection: "When you come to work here, the biggest challenge is learning which mug is whose. Then you've got to memorize where it's hanging, so you can grab it fast and have it filled and on the table before its owner hits the seat."

Clear-Broth Clam Chowder

"The trouble with most people's chowder is they cook it too long," Flo Klewin believes. "It gets too strong. Take it off the heat fast, if you want it to be nice." We have reduced the measurements in her Kitchen Little recipe, which calls for a gallon of clams, but we have maintained the fundamental technique of simmering the chowder a mere three minutes once the clams are added. The result is a gentle-flavored broth.

4 slices thick bacon (about ¼ pound)	18–20 large, hard-shell clams (quahogs), shucked and drained, and their liquor
2 cups chopped onion	
1 pound red boiling potatoes	Black pepper
3 cups bottled clam liquor (juice)	¼ cup fresh basil, chopped

1. Cut the bacon into 1-inch pieces. Fry it in a large pot until crisp. Remove the bacon pieces and save them to put in omelets tomorrow morning.

2. Add chopped onions to the rendered bacon fat, and sauté them until soft.

3. Add potatoes, bottled clam liquor, and enough water to fully cover the potatoes. Bring to a boil, cover, and simmer, 12 minutes, or until potatoes are tender.

4. Coarsely chop the clams with a knife (do not mince or use a food processor). You should have about three cups of clam meat.

5. Strain the clam liquor through a double layer of cheesecloth to remove impurities or boil it and skim off the foam that rises to the top.

6. Add the clams and clam liquor to the chowder pot. Bring it back to a boil. Simmer three minutes.

7. Remove from heat. Add black pepper to taste. Sprinkle on basil. Serve with crackers.

Makes 6–8 servings.

Lasyone's Meat Pie Kitchen & Restaurant

NATCHITOCHES, LOUISIANA

ames Lasyone (whose last name rhymes with *jazzy-bone*), remembers that, a quarter of a century ago, if you wanted to buy a meat pie in Natchitoches (pronounced *nack-uh-tush*), you needed to cozy up to one of the town ladies who prepared the savory local delights in her home kitchen for sale to the public. If you didn't know a pie maker, and were not on her preferred customer list, you didn't have a prayer. "She might take care of you if you were recommended by a regular patron," Mr. Lasyone explains. "But those ladies just didn't make pies for anyone who called on them." This deeply disturbed Mr. Lasyone, who grew up in the farmland outside the old river community and remembered meat pies as one of the fundamental foods of his youth. He tells of the days when they were sold on street corners from white baby buggies, pushed by little boys who would chant to advertise the freshness and good taste of their victuals, and who kept their pies warm with a small wood fire, perfuming the avenues of town with the fragrance of seasoned beef in a pastry crust.

"I cannot explain for certain how meat pies first came to this place," Mr. Lasyone says, suggesting that it might have happened well over a century ago, when Natchitoches—founded in 1714, it is the oldest settlement in the Louisiana Purchase—was a thriving trade center and outfitting point for settlers heading west. It is possible, he speculates, that the meat pie made its appearance in those days before the Red River shifted course away from town. "I feel that the pies must have arrived when they herded those cattle through the dirt streets to the river and loaded them on boats. I believe it was cooks on the boats from faraway who made the meat pies. People in town liked them, learned how to make them, and never forgot them."

By the midtwentieth century, however, street-corner pie vendors were fading into history. James Lasyone, who had grown up a sharecropper's son and had enjoyed the pies when his family came to town, became the butcher at a grocery store on Second Street. When he wanted a meat pie, he knew which ladies to call. "Some were white, some were black," he remembers, "but there weren't many of them left." In the mid-1960s, he began experimenting with recipes to make his own pies. He sold some over the butcher's counter at the store, then, in 1967, he opened Lasyone's Meat Pie Kitchen in a minuscule retail space near the meat market that had been home to a finance company office. You could buy his meat pies to take home and fry, and he also made some on premises, ready to eat.

"See that little old pot over there," he says, pointing to a black fry kettle displayed on a shelf in the dining room of his restaurant. "That's all I started with. That, and a six dollar and ninety-five cent investment in groceries."

As prepared by Mr. Lasyone, a meat pie is a half-circle-shaped pastry pocket about the size of a taco, with a rugged crimp around its edges. It has a golden crust that is brittle near the crimp, soft at its mounded center. Inside is seasoned ground beef, moist enough to make gravy irrelevant.

Spicy but not fiery, complex and succulent, Mr. Lasyone's meat pie is an honest piece of food that satisfies in an old-fashioned way. You can get one for breakfast, accompanied by eggs and hash browns; most steady customers come midday to get a pair of them for lunch, with soulful dirty rice on the side, darkened with plenty of gizzards and topped with zesty gravy.

The pleasure of a meal at Lasyone's is amplified by the history that pervades town. Nearby Front Street, facing the banks of clear Cane River Lake where paddle-wheelers once docked, is still paved with bricks and lined with shops that have upper-level porches festooned with lacy, wrought-iron fleurs-de-lis. The antebellum plantation homes and gardens around Natchitoches are some of the most beautiful in the South. In this environment, a meat pie at Lasyone's has the taste of edible history. (At the annual Natchitoches-Northwestern State University Folk Festival in July, Mr. Lasyone sells thousands of his meat pies. Not only are they excellent fair food, wieldy enough to eat without utensils, but they are also authentic folk food.)

While meat pies are its main claim to fame, Lasyone's is also an exemplary place to savor all manner of regional delights. Some dishes are enthusiastically spiced to reflect the French and Spanish traditions on which Creole cookery was built; in addition to these brightly seasoned specialties, the menu always lists a delectable roster of southern hallmarks from biscuits and grits in the morning to crisp-fried catfish and chicken-and-dumpling stew at noon. Many local customers, apparently aloof to the allure of the meat pie, come to Lasyone's simply because it is the best place in town for a quick, inexpensive meal in a pleasant setting: hot lunch, such as liver smothered with onions or a brace of chicken-fried steaks with plenty of gravy, or a breakfast of ham (available sliced thick or thin) and eggs, with hot grits on the side.

Mr. Lasyone is the kind of chef who delights in creating things. When we spoke with him, he was in the midst of developing a chicken-and-spaghetti dish. "I have three good recipes," he said, "but not one of them is exactly right. So, I'm taking a little of this from that one, and a little of that from this one, and I think I'll come up with one that is exactly right."

A robust man, who clearly has little trouble enjoying food, Mr. Lasyone attributes his culinary skills to his mother. When he was growing up,

Indiana, years ago: These words are a siren song to fans of roadfood

Every Autumn, Hatch, New Mexico holds a town-wide chile festival.
Here, Jane clings to the sign on the road into town.

A between-meal hobby for us is shopping in prison gift stores

A roadside stand in the back of a truck: Buy your chiles raw or roasted

RIGHT: Chile *ristras* (ropes) can be decorative as well as edible

BELOW: Just-harvested chile peppers on their way to market in New Mexico's Mesilla Valley

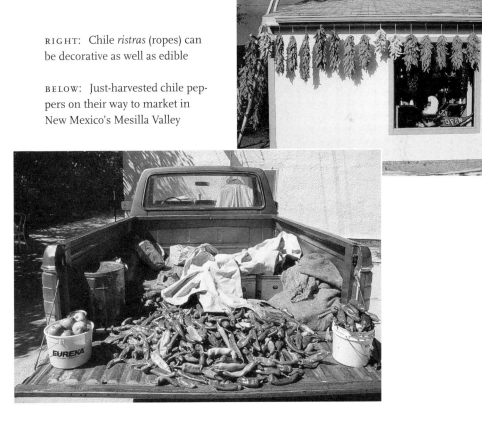

This is us in 1999. We bought some grand put-up preserves at a store in Turkey, Texas.

Arnold Burgers made a specialty of meals to go; hence the legs on these speedy sandwiches

Pie is one of the traveling eater's basic food groups

Roadside Wisconsin: The Dairy State

Connie's, on the west side of Chicago, served awesome sausage sandwiches

The Hollywood Café, in the Mississippi Delta, claims to have invented the fried dill pickle

LEFT: Aside from fantastic food, Memphis is a city of inspired signage. This folk-art illustration was on the side of a café that served fire-hot barbecue.

BELOW: We bought this sign from the proprietor of the Four Way Grill, a soul-food restaurant in Memphis

ABOVE: We tend to eat breakfast in the morning, but it's nice to know it is always there

RIGHT: Like the earliest of diners, converted school buses tend to be great sources of blue-plate chow

Is it ever *not* time to eat? We found this sign on a Pennsylvania diner in 1976.

We did like this café's service, food, coffee, and prices.
Alas, it closed when a fast-food franchise moved next door.

"What'll ya' have, hon'?": The Country Diner, Clayton, North Carolina, 1978

he recalls, he and his siblings used to catch rabbits and bring them to her for supper. They watched how she dressed their catch and cooked it over an open fire, near the kettle where she did her wash. "Your food choices are limited when you are a sharecropper," he says. "So, you learn to invent things; you develop the habit of making the most of what you have. To be a good cook, you have to want to create something when you see a handful of ingredients."

To illustrate his point, he tells how, not long ago, he invented Cane River pie, a dessert that has become nearly as renowned as his meat pie. "One day I was making twenty-two strawberry shortcakes. I had all my ingredients lined up on the counter, but someone in the kitchen had left a glass of chocolate milk nearby. I accidentally poured it in the batter. At first I was mad, but then I thought, *this is interesting.* After that, I fiddled and I fussed, and I played with the idea, and I believe I finally got it right."

The Cane River cream pie that ultimately resulted from his experiments has no chocolate milk in the batter, but it does have chocolate sauce poured on top of two layers of gingerbread that sandwich a thin layer of custard. The sauce seeps into the cake and creates fudgy streaks in the gingerbread. A slice of Cane River pie vaguely resembles a Boston cream pie, but one that is dark and spicy and wickedly sweet—a set of qualities especially well suited to the conclusion of a meal in the bayous of Louisiana.

Natchitoches Meat Pie

Like so many things in this part of the world, James Lasyone's recipes are top-secret.
Our recipe for meat pie is loosely based on one in the Cane River Cuisine *cookbook,*

published by the women of the Service League of Natchitoches in 1974. It was sub-mitted by Mrs. Charles E. Cloutier.

6 ounces ground beef

6 ounces ground pork

$^{1}/_{3}$ cup chopped green onions, tops and stems

1 tablespoon salt

$^{1}/_{4}$ teaspoon coarsely ground black pepper

$^{1}/_{4}$ teaspoon red-pepper flakes

$^{1}/_{4}$ teaspoon cayenne pepper

3 tablespoons all-purpose flour

CRUST

4 cups flour

1 teaspoon salt

1 teaspoon baking powder

$^{1}/_{2}$ cup cold Crisco or other solid veg-etable shortening, not melted

1 egg, beaten

1 cup milk

Oil, for deep frying

1. Combine beef, pork, onions, salt, and peppers in a heavy skillet. Cook over medium heat, stirring to keep it from clumping, until meat is cooked through. Do not overcook. Sift 3 tablespoons flour over the meat, stirring well. Remove from heat and cool to room temperature. Drain any fat from skillet.

2. To make crust, sift together flour, salt, and baking powder. Cut in short-ening, until mixture resembles coarse meal. Stir in beaten egg and milk. Form dough into a ball. Roll out $^{1}/_{3}$ of the dough and cut it into 5 $^{1}/_{2}$-inch circles. (Mrs. Cloutier says she uses the top of an old coffee pot as a cutter.) Roll out and cut the remaining two-thirds of the dough, keeping the circles on a cookie sheet, separated by waxed paper.

3. To assemble the pies, place a heaping tablespoon slightly off center onto each pastry circle. Dampen the edge of the pie containing the meat with your fingertips, fold over the meat, and crimp with a fork dipped in water. Use the fork to prick the folded-over pastry once or twice.

4. Fry pies, a few at a time, in a deep kettle, at 350°F, until golden brown. Drain on paper towels. Serve immediately.

Makes 10–12 pies.
(Cocktail-sized meat pies can be made by cutting smaller circles and using less filling.)

Lusco's

GREENWOOD, MISSISSIPPI

*L*usco's of Greenwood is as truly and deeply southern as any place on earth: shabby, but unmistakably elegant; hidebound, yet unashamed to adopt modern conveniences, like the single-portion plastic tubs of oleomargarine they now serve instead of butter. Of course, there is a good reason Lusco's gave up butter. Nothing happens here by accident, explains Karen Pinkston, a third-generation Lusco by marriage. She reveals that the margarine is on the table to thwart the butter flippers. But, before we get too deep into the butter-pat issue, let us tell you why this strange restaurant is so beloved by citizens of the Delta.

It is old, which is automatically good in Mississippi. Cotton planters around Greenwood came to know Charles "Papa" Lusco in the 1920s, when he drove a horsedrawn grocery wagon to their plantations, bringing supplies from the market he and Marie "Mama" Lusco ran. Mama sold plates of her spaghetti at the store, and Papa built secret dining rooms in back, where customers could enjoy his homemade wine with their meals. Even after Prohibition, the clandestine cubicles remained, giving Lusco's a seductively covert character that has endeared it to generations of local gentry. During World War II, the back rooms became a favorite haunt of soldiers stationed at nearby bases, and they spread Lusco's notoriety as a place to eat well, drink freely, and act rowdy behind the privacy of curtained booths.

Greenwood, Cotton Capital of the World, is itself a sight. At harvest time in fall, the roadsides all around are strewn with white fluff, blown off trucks carrying just-picked bales. Lusco's is in a tumbledown part of town that brims with local color; its neighbors include an ancient, striped-pole barber shop where patriarchs in overalls philosophize on a bench just outside; dress shops selling ladies' fashions that appear unchanged since 1961; used furniture stores with grandiose dining-room suites taken from down-on-their-luck plantation houses; an aromatic deep-fried catfish joint; and a few ghostly reupholstery shops. Lusco's shares its storefront with the office of the L.C.M.C. Memorial Gardens Cemetery.

You might think you have entered the wrong place when you walk in the front door. Lusco's does not look like a restaurant, nor does it look much like a grocery store or any other known type of business establishment. All you can say for certain is that it is threadbare and odd, qualities that endear it to the local clientele. The walls of a big, wood-floored vestibule are painted institutional green, and festooned with small game trophies. In one corner, some waiting-room chairs and a

couch are arranged around a television set and an old kiosk with a pay phone inside. At busy mealtimes, people wait around the TV and phone booth or on stools at a defunct short-order counter until their room and table in back become available. The private dining carrels are arranged off dim hallways, where the decor includes a story written on a placemat by Delta chronicler Willie Morris, a signed picture from the bearded guys of ZZ Top, and photographs of Art Linkletter and Paul Harvey when each came here to dine. The interiors of the booths are concealed by heavy old curtains, so, although you can hear other customers (the partitions don't go all the way to the ceiling), you see no one but your dining companions, across a field of luxurious white cotton cloth and thick folded napkins. These eating areas might be fine lovers' hideaways if the weak lighting and pastel walls didn't cast a tubercular pea-green hue across everybody's face. The effect is more eerie than it is romantic, and there is something a little silly about those moments when the curtain gets pulled aside and a member of the staff peers in to inquire if everything is satisfactory. To summon service in your dining carrel, each booth is equipped with a buzzer.

If you are an old customer of Lusco's, returning after several years away, you will be shocked by the changes. First, you'll get a menu. The kitchen's repertoire is no longer called out by a waiter. That's too bad, because it used to be a thrill when one of the old-timers swept back the curtain and began to rhapsodize about "T-bone steak tender as a mother's love" and broiled shrimp with sauce available in degrees of spicyness described as "hot or hot-eee!" These venerable gentlemen, who had worked at Lusco's for decades, are now mostly retired, their places taken by a younger, pert waitstaff. The new people are pleasant and helpful, but they lack their predecessors' vintage antebellum manners, as well as their facility for memorizing the bill of fare every day, so they issue a menu and describe only daily specials.

The other big change at Lusco's is the tin ceiling: It is clean. Butter pats aren't stuck there any more. For several decades, the Lusco's dining experience used to include not only lusty eating and drinking, but also seeing how adept one was at using flatware to catapult pats of butter upwards and making them stick. "You'd be surprised who used to do that," Karen Pinkston confides. "It wasn't children, it wasn't teenagers or drunken sailors. It was well-bred southern ladies and gentlemen. They would get to yelling and screaming in one of the back rooms and pretty soon the butter would go flying. It became a problem in the winter, when we turned on the heat. Heat rises, so the butter melted. I paid many cleaning bills, and had some men with no hair who got their scalps dripped on and said they would never come back." In 1989, the health department insisted something be done. "The older butter had been up there for years," Karen admitted. "Some of it had petrified. There were teams of men on scaffolds scraping hard for two weeks to clean the ceiling, and the painter said, 'Please, don't ever call me again!'" A sign in the waiting area now warns that butter throwing is classified under law as malicious mischief—a moot point, considering that butter pats are no longer served at Lusco's.

Even with its butterless ceiling, Lusco's is weird. "People who come here, regardless of where they have lived, have never seen anything like it," Karen Pinkston says. No doubt, strangeness has enhanced its reputation, particularly here in the heart of Mississippi, where eccentricity is treasured, but the main reason for its renown is deluxe Delta food. Mama and Papa Lusco were Italian by way of Louisiana, so the flavors of the kitchen they established are as much Creole as they are southern or Italian. Gumbo, crab, and shrimp are always on the menu, and oysters are a specialty in season—on the half shell or baked with bacon. Because so many regular patrons have always been big spenders from well-to-do cotton families, the menu is best known among them for its high-end items. Lusco's T-bone steaks are some of the finest anywhere: sumptuous cuts that are brought raw to the table for your approval, then broiled to pillowy succulence. Pompano has for many years been a house trademark: broiled and served whole, bathed in a magical sauce made of butter, lemon, and secret spices.

Getting perfect pompano is a constant problem for Andy Pinkston, Papa Lusco's grandson and inheritor of the kitchen. He explains that pompano from the east or west coast simply isn't as fine as that from the Gulf, the meat of which is delicate-textured, pearly white, and sweet. When he cannot get the best pompano, he sells none at all. About ten summers ago, when we stopped by to eat, there was graffiti on the wall of the men's room (which is out the back door) that read, The Great Depression of '84: Lusco's has no pompano. February through May are the months when the Pinkstons are most likely to obtain a supply of the aristocratic fish but, the rest of the year, they frequently compensate for its absence by serving small trout, prepared whole and swimming in the tasty fish sauce, with its bones removed.

The sauce for Lusco's broiled shrimp is nearly as far famed as that used on pompano and trout. Firm, plump crescents are served in a silky, translucent bath of buttery juice that has the zing of vinegar and pepper, and also a fusillade of strange, beguiling spices (could that be cardamom

we taste?). Whatever the ingredients, Karen and Andy Pinkston won't tell a soul. Mystery is a byword in this part of the world, and secrets are fundamental to the character of Lusco's. The broiled-shrimp sauce is available in hot or mild variations, and it is possible to get the shrimp either plain or heaped with hunks of milk-white crabmeat; you can also have crabmeat alone, served in fish sauce or shrimp sauce. Lusco's menu always lists gumbo, and it is usually a gallimaufry of different seafoods. Last time we visited, though, Andy Pinkston had made an authoritative crawfish gumbo: peppery and perfumed with deep smoky character, loaded with crawfish and spoonfuls of slippery, fresh okra.

Ordinary spaghetti is no longer regularly made at Lusco's; instead, the kitchen offers interesting pastas. One night, angelhair noodles are available with shrimp and crabmeat and a measure of piquant shrimp sauce. Or there are mezzi rigatoni—stout, square noodles in red meat sauce. The sauce, which is here referred to by its old Italian-American name, "gravy," is a sweet, chunky brew flavored with savory shreds of well-cooked beefsteak that Andy Pinkston puts aside when he trims his ribeyes and T-bones.

Lusco's has long been known for its New Orleans-style salad of iceberg lettuce dolled up with anchovies, capers, and olives, and liberally sopped in a fragrant vinaigrette, but Karen Pinkston is a serious salad buff who has made it her business to add more modern alternatives. One evening's choices included Mediterranean salad, made with feta cheese; traditional Caesar salad; and a salad billed as Gourmet's Delight, made with arugula, radicchio, endive, red lettuce, and spinach. "Andy likes to tease me about that one," Karen says about the latter. "He tells me it's just weeds I've picked by the side of the highway. But, the fact is, the Delta is different now than it used to be, and the new people have more educated palates. Even this place has to change with the times."

Karen allows that one thing will never change about the old dowager of a restaurant she and her husband tend: "It is required that no one does the cooking but a member of the family. Andy and I do it all. This is Lusco's, after all, and when people come to dine with us, they have a right to expect only Luscos in the kitchen."

Lusco's Fish Sauce (Not)

You can buy a bottle of Lusco's fish sauce at the restaurant and, although the Pinkstons are not really set up for mail-order sales, they will sell bottles by the case if you call and twist their arms. Still, students at Karen Pinkston's cooking class demanded to know Lusco's famous recipe, which, of course, she had no intention of disclosing. Instead, she and Andy concocted this "lemon-butter sauce" recipe, which, when combined with a nearly equal amount of melted margarine (not butter), closely approximates what is served over pompano and trout at the restaurant. Mysteries and margarine aside, this recipe makes a fine, simple topping for almost any flatfish, whole or fileted.

½ cup melted butter

1 clove garlic, minced

½ teaspoon salt

½ teaspoon freshly ground black pepper

¼ cup lemon juice

Combine all the ingredients and heat through. Pour liberally over portions of cooked fish.

Makes enough sauce for 4 servings (or, when combined with margarine, 6–8).

Ma Groover's Pig and Plate

VALDOSTA, GEORGIA

*M*a Groover opened her café in Valdosta, not far from Moody Air Force Base, in 1935, during the Great Depression. For more than four decades, in bad times and good, she served wonderful, inexpensive home cooking to flyboys, locals, and lucky passers-by—three meals a day, seven days a week.

She called what she served "just farm cooking" because it was on the family farm that she learned to cook, as a little girl, at her mother's side. The main courses best remembered by frequent customers include chicken and dumplings, pork chops with cornbread dressing, catfish and hushpuppies, and smoked Florida mullet. Every morning, Ma wrote out a menu that listed what she planned to cook that day. She rotated entrees for the sake of regulars who came for lunch nearly every day, and she based her vegetable selection on what was fresh in the market when she stopped there on the way to the restaurant.

How well we recall our first visit back in the mid-1970s, when we were so dazzled by the menu choices that Ma felt compelled to give us a helping hand. "You look like the kind who would like my smoked mullet," she said, pointing an arthritic finger at Michael. "And you," she said, sizing up Jane correctly, "You look like baked chicken and dumplings."

As for the vegetable selection, she lovingly described eight or ten from which we could choose. They included cooked-soft rutabagas, sweet potato soufflé, pole beans, squash casserole, buttered corn on the cob, greens sopped with pot likker, blackeyed peas, and macaroni and cheese. On the table to accompany our Dixie feasts was a basket of cracklin' cornbread muffins. Ma told us that any cracklin' cornbread not served that day would find its way into dressing to accompany the next day's pork chops.

When Ma gave us the recipe for cracklin' bread, we told her that where we live, up north, cracklin's (bits of roasted pig skin) were hard to come by. So she suggested that in a pinch we could use well-cooked, thick-sliced bacon instead of cracklin's. If you are anywhere in the south where barbecued pork is popular, you should be able to find cracklin's in a barbecue parlor. Otherwise, bacon does provide a good, piggy savor.

Cracklin' Cornbread Muffins

1½ cups yellow cornmeal

½ cup flour

1 tablespoon baking powder

½ teaspoon salt

3 eggs

1 cup milk

5 tablespoons butter, melted and cooled, plus additional, for greasing

½ pound cracklin's or cooked bacon, diced

1. Grease 16 muffin cups very generously with one tablespoon of butter and put the muffin tin in an oven. Turn the oven up to 400°F, and allow the grease to melt in the cups as you prepare the batter and the oven heats.

2. Combine cornmeal, flour, baking powder, and salt in a large mixing bowl.

3. Mix eggs and milk in a separate bowl.

4. Make a well in the center of the dry ingredients. Add the milk-egg mixture and blend using as few strokes as possible—10 to 15, max. Stir in melted butter and cracklin's, mixing only until barely blended.

5. Ladle the batter into the hot muffin cups about $^2/_3$ full. Bake 15–20 minutes, until golden brown.

6. Turn muffins onto a rack to cool. Serve warm.

Makes 12–15 muffins.

Mama Lo's

*A*bout thirty years ago, Lorene (Mama Lo) Alexander opened a soul food restaurant in a whitewashed cinderblock building, near the police station in Gainesville. Every morning, she went to the market to buy vegetables, and back at her café she set the collards boiling, the squash steaming, the corn frying, and the eggplant baking; she then sat down to hand write a few copies of the day's menu. They were inscribed with a ballpoint pen on a piece of blue-lined notebook paper, and they were passed around the dining room until closing, by which time they were limp and wrinkled, smudged, stained, and torn. The exhausted menus were thrown away at the end of lunch hour, and the next morning, new ones were written.

Mama Lo's closed in the mid-1990s, by which time she had become a folk hero among students at the nearby University of Florida, officers of the Gainesville police force, and a few canny travelers who marked her place on their maps as a citadel of downhome cooking in north Florida.

It was as unpretentious an eatery as you could find anywhere. Above the door of the bunkerlike building, a small neon sign said simply, *Mama Lo's*. Inside, there were two wood-paneled rooms—one with a pool table, a jukebox, and an arcade game; the other with a scattering of tables. You could not spend more than five dollars for a meal.

What you got for your money in this plebeian setting was a royal feast. For a main course, you could choose from among fried chicken, chicken and dumplings, chicken and yellow rice, smoked sausage and syrup-sweet yams, stuffed pork chops, stuffed bell peppers, chitlin's, meat loaf, or fried fish. The vegetable list was always an awesome twelve to eighteen items long. Year around, you could count on mustard or collard greens sopped in high-seasoned potlikker, okra-tomato-corn succotash, potatoes and rice of all kinds, lima beans, and buttered carrots.

And, of course, with every meal, there was cornbread. For dessert, Mama Lo made poundcake, coconut cake, and peach shortcake.

Although we did love her pork chops, our favorite thing to eat at Mama Lo's was an all-vegetable dinner. Each veggie was served in its own separate little dish. With that cornbread on the side, a selection of three or four made for an exhilarating meatless meal. The most spectacular of the vegetable dishes were the casseroles. Mama Lo's eggplant soufflé was a kitchen miracle that turned the common southern side dish into a taste

sensation. Her broccoli casserole magically transformed the dour stalks of green into something rich, sweet, and satisfying by combining them with a luxurious and ultrasoulful melange of eggs, cheese, sugar, and cushiony white bread. Although it is a side dish, Mama Lo's broccoli casserole is a taste-and-texture wonderland, packing enough variety to seem like a complete meal. It will serve four to six people as a side dish, but we make a batch to split (with a tiny bit left over for the next day), whenever we are in desperate need of culinary comfort.

Mama Lo's Broccoli Casserole

5–6 slices white bread, torn into
bite–sized pieces

1 bunch broccoli

3 eggs

¹/₄ cup milk

4 tablespoons butter, melted, plus
additional, for greasing

1 cup grated cheddar cheese

1 teaspoon salt

3 tablespoons sugar

1. Preheat oven to 350°F.

2. Grease an 8-inch-square Pyrex baking dish. Cover bottom of dish generously with torn bread. Cut broccoli (head and tops of stems) into bite-sized pieces and lay on top of bread.

3. Mix all remaining ingredients. Pour over broccoli and bread.

4. Cover with aluminum foil. Bake, 35 minutes. For a chewier top, remove foil during the last 10–12 minutes of baking.

Makes 6 servings.

Mamie's

*T*here are a few dozen varieties of cornbread in the South; it is rare to come across a real southern restaurant that doesn't serve it in some form. Basic cornbread is baked as individual rolls or in muffin tins, with or without cracklin's (chewy nuggets of baconlike pig meat), jalapeño peppers, or shredded cheddar cheese. There are also corn dodgers, hushpuppies, and corn sticks cooked in old-fashioned tins that yield fat tubes of bread that resemble miniature ears of corn. And there are innumerable varieties of spoonbread, which is a soufflélike "bread" served with a spoon and eaten with a fork.

One of our favorite varieties is served in Tennessee and parts of Kentucky. It usually goes by the plain and generic name *cornbread*, giving unsuspecting customers no clue that they have a special treat in store when they order it. This kind of cornbread is made from a batter poured onto a well-greased grill, and is essentially a big, steamy pancake, but served at the noon meal instead of in the morning. It is a fine companion for baked ham, catfish, or fried chicken, and especially for country-fried steak, or any gravy-topped dish that makes you need something to mop up extra gravy from the plate.

This cornbread, also known as *corn cake*, is best when served hot off the griddle in a fast-moving cafeteria line, so that a glob of margarine or butter set atop it is half-melted by the time you get your tray to a table in the dining room. You can eat it politely with a fork, or you can tear off pieces and use them to dip in a dish of turnip greens and potlikker.

One of the greatest places to eat such cornbread was a small cafeteria in Memphis, known as Mamie's, named after its founder and chef, Mamie Gammon. Mamie was something of a culinary legend in Memphis (which is like being a god on Mount Olympus), known especially for her prowess with such southern-style vegetables as candied yams, beets in orange sauce, powerhouse turnip greens, and her own version of dirty rice, enriched with giblets. She made a mighty meatloaf, four-star fried chicken, featherweight dinner rolls, and superb banana pudding and fried apple or peach pies, for dessert. Whatever else she served at her little cafeteria, you could almost always count on corn cakes—hot and toothsome, a great companion to a full meal or a simple bowl of vegetables.

Mamie's is gone, but this good recipe for corn cakes is a reminder of the glory that used to be.

Tennessee Cornbread – Pancake

2 eggs, well beaten
1 cup buttermilk
1/2 cup milk
1 cup white cornmeal
1 cup all-purpose flour

1/2 teaspoon baking soda
1/2 teaspoon salt
1/2 cup water (approximate)
Butter or margarine, for frying

1. Combine all ingredients in order listed, adding just enough water to get a batter that is like pancake batter—pourable but not too thin.

2. Melt a generous amount of butter on a griddle or in a large skillet over medium heat. Pour out batter to create 4-inch diameter cakes. Fry until light brown. Turn and fry other side, adding more butter, if necessary. Continue until all batter is used.

3. Serve immediately, topped with pats of butter or margarine.

Makes 12 corn cakes, serving 4–6.

Manny's Coffee Shop

CHICAGO, ILLINOIS

*A*t Manny's, even if you don't come to eat with your friends, associates, attorney, parole officer, alderman, or image consultant, you are never really alone. Seating is perforce communal, and regulars feel free to hobnob loudly with each other even if they are four tables apart. Proprietor Ken Raskin, son of the late Manny, works the rooms, greeting chowhounds who have known him since he was a small boy. Arlene (Ken's mother, Manny's widow, and now a bride [her husband Larry Mann is a longtime Manny's customer]), often spends the noon hour making the rounds to make sure all is right with the world. "Isn't it nice to see how well they're eating?" Arlene asks one day as she gazes over the restaurant with all the pride of a Jewish mother who has fashioned every matzoh ball and kreplach with her own hands. "That's what I like to see: clean plates and happy faces."

So, who are the happy ladies and gentlemen cleaning their plates at Manny's?

Three executives from a meat-packing company share a table, heralding what's in their sandwiches as "the best, freshest, most consistent meat in the city—the real thing, and nothing but." Each man has slung his tie over his left shoulder to ensure that the neckwear doesn't get splattered with julienne salad, juices from sliced brisket, knish crumbs, or shreds of corned beef and pastrami. "It's the Manny's way," one explains, putting his fingers inside the front apron of his tie and wiggling it like a puppet.

Raymond Sloan, who operates a business nearby, has been a steady customer since the first Mayor Daley's reign. He brags that he has eaten lunch at Manny's five days a week for the last twelve years, and has never had the exact same meal twice. Mr. Sloan, who is seventy-four, says, "Today, I had tuna salad and lemonade. I like the gefilte fish, the spaghetti, and, occasionally, the brisket of beef. I love the corned beef, but, unfortunately, it doesn't like me." He especially enjoys entertaining clients at Manny's bare tables under the bright fluorescent lights. "My Japanese associates are thrilled to come. When I tell them where we're going, they say 'C.B. on rye!'"

Milly Kovan trekked to Manny's from Farmington Hills, Michigan. "This is such a flavor of Chicago," she says. "You don't eat fancy. You eat good. I was moving along the line and, when I saw that corned beef piled up, I decided that for once in my life I would order exactly what I want. Corned beef it was. On rye. With latkes, too!" Mrs. Kovan is seated at an especially large table with six couples who all met a while ago at the Racquet Club in Scottsdale, Arizona, and decided to have a Chicago reunion.

Bernie Josephs, introduced to us by Arlene as "the King of Foam Rubber," is far and away the most dapper man in the restaurant. A Manny's regular, he always sports an outfit in which one astonishing color is celebrated neck to toe. We meet him on powder-blue day: blue jacket and beltless slacks with socks to match, striped pale blue shirt and tie, and a silk pocket square blooming from his chest in a darker blue, for contrast. On the opposite lapel is a Rotary Club pin awarded for decades of service. "I have been coming to Manny's for over thirty years," he proclaims. "The Salisbury steak is, to me, revered. Corned beef? The doctor said it isn't good for me, but I must have my corned beef fix once every two weeks, or else I cannot function. So, I brought my doctor here one day. Now he's a regular customer."

"Along with the famous, we get the infamous," Ken Raskin says with a bit of a blush. "You know, those on the other side of the law. I remember one time we had a table of them sitting at lunch, when a group of detectives walked in. I didn't notice anything until I heard the back-door alarm sound. The gangsters had gotten up and run out the rear, but they left money on the dishwashing machine in the kitchen to pay for their lunch. I guess they were honest crooks."

Manny's regulars arrange their gastronomic life based on a schedule of daily specials that almost never changes. Monday, you can count on corned-beef hash, stuffed green peppers, and breaded veal chops.

Wednesday is the day for chicken pot pie or turkey drumsticks and mushroom-barley soup. Friday is fried smelts, perch, and macaroni day. Thursday is the most thrilling day of the week for a large coterie of oxtail-stew aficionados, because Ken makes only a certain amount (limited by

the size of the pot). "We bring it out at nine-thirty in the morning," he says, "and, by noon, it's gone. They fight for it. They call ahead to reserve an order. They come in during coffee break and get some to take back to work for lunch."

Recipes are old ones, some going back fifty years, to when brothers Jack and Charlie Raskin, sons of Russian-Roumanian immigrants, opened their first cafeteria on Halstead Street. Their specialty was nonkosher Jewish cooking, served quickly, in large portions—the way Charlie had learned by watching his mother. In Manny's kitchen today, matzoh balls are still enriched with real *schmaltz* (chicken fat); gefilte fish is always freshly made. Beef arrives in steamship rounds, which Ken says he buys partly because customers like to see the big haunch of beef sliced at the sandwich counter, but also because he uses all its byproducts. "The bones are for beef stock; the fat we render down and use to sauté onions; the trimmings are for hamburgers and meat loaf. I don't like to buy ground beef; you don't know what's in it. We also need the leftovers from the cooked beef to make kreplach and knishes." He apologizes for today's borscht, which he feels might be a little too sweet, but the pound cake, which he makes each morning when he arrives at three-thirty, is especially luxurious and to his liking.

Manny's began shortly after World War II, when the Raskin brothers split up so Jack could buy his own restaurant on Roosevelt Road near the open-air market area called Maxwell Street. It was a shoestring operation at first, with Jack's teenage son Emmanuel, who had learned by watching his uncle, serving as the cook. The restaurant Jack bought used to be named Sunny's. So, rather than tear down the old sign and buy a whole new one, Jack named it after his boy, saving money by simply buying two letters and replacing the *Su* in *Sunny's* with *Ma*. The address changed a few times after that, then, in 1964, Manny's moved to the current spot on Jefferson. Ken remembers his father saying, "I know what the people in this neighborhood want, and I am the only one left who can do it."

Unless you work in downtown Chicago or are enough of a bargain hunter to enjoy scouring the job-lot shops, outlets, discount stores, and bargain bins of the neighborhood, Manny's isn't all that convenient to reach. Eager investors have approached Ken Raskin suggesting he open a "Manny's North" in a place amenable to a more upscale clientele. "I couldn't do that," Ken explains. "Because I couldn't be two places at once. What they don't understand is this: You cannot have a Manny's without Manny being here. When my father passed away, ten years ago, some of the old timers grumbled that it would never be the same again because he was gone. But they've stopped muttering, and now a lot of them have begun to call me Manny. That's fine with me. It's a good name."

Farmer's Chop Suey

No one knows how this simple dairy salad came to be, but it has been a hot-weather favorite in Jewish-American kitchens for at least a century, and, at Manny's, it is always available during heat waves. Served with good pumpernickel or rye bread, it is a light, satisfying summer lunch.

1 bunch radishes, sliced thin

2 small cucumbers, sliced thin

1 bunch diced scallions, including tops

2 cups sour cream

1 large tomato, cut into bite-sized cubes

Salt and pepper, to taste

2 cups farmer cheese, pot cheese, or dry-curd cottage cheese (optional)

Combine radishes, cucumbers, and scallions with sour cream. Gently fold in tomatoes. Season to taste. Serve chilled. For a more substantial salad, serve atop a mound of pot cheese, farmer cheese, or cottage cheese.

Makes 4 servings.

Potato Latkes

1–2 baking potato (about $3/4$ pound total)

$1/4$ cup grated onion

2 eggs, beaten

1 teaspoon salt

$1/4$ teaspoon black pepper

1 tablespoon flour

$1/8$ teaspoon baking powder

$1/4$ cup butter

Vegetable oil, for frying

Sour cream and/or applesauce

1. Peel and grate potatoes. You will need about 2 cups. In a colander, combine potatoes with onions, and press out as much moisture as you can. Put the potato mixture in a bowl and mix it with eggs, salt, pepper, flour, and baking powder. Let stand, 5 minutes.

2. Heat the butter and about $1/4$-inch vegetable oil in a heavy skillet, until hot but not smoking. Drop pancake mixture into oil in 2-tablespoon portions. Use a wooden spoon to press the mixture flat (but not *too* flat). Do not crowd the pan. Fry each pancake, about 2 minutes, until golden brown; flip and fry the other side, about 1 minute. Remove with a slotted spoon and drain on paper towels.

3. Serve latkes immediately. Sour cream and/or apple sauce are the proper condiments.

Makes about 10 latkes.

McClard's Bar-B-2

S tarted in 1928, with a precious recipe that Alex and Gladys McClard accepted in lieu of rent from a tenant at their Hot Springs tourist court, McClard's has become Arkansas's premier house of barbecue. To call the old, whitewashed-stucco building a busy operation does not begin to describe the ebullience of the place every evening as barbecue hounds line up at all three different entryways waiting for an open table or counter seats. There is no organized wait list and no hostess to regulate traffic; regulars know to grab a booth when one opens up, and amazingly, the oddball nonsystem works. There can be a certain amount of hungry hovering—the overly eager muscling through a door and toward a table where customers look like they are almost finished eating—but even the hungriest hoverers appear polite enough to hold back until the table is actually vacated.

Through the pandemonium shoulder McClard's veteran waitresses, toting plates piled high with smoke-perfumed pork. "Didn't I know you when I was a child?" asks one middle-aged woman who has managed to secure a booth with her husband and two teenage boys.

"Yes," says Wynona, a good ol' gal with thirty-five years of waitressing under her belt, and a talent for pushing through the dining room like a Razorback lineman. "I used to bring you half-spreads."

"Why, that's right!" the woman says with utter amazement. But Wynona hasn't time to chit-chat. She delivers the family's spreads and ribs, then goes on her way to bring more barbecue to other hungry customers.

What is a spread? Good question! A spread is McClard's name for a tamale plate, a Hot Springs echo of the Mississippi River Delta's fondness for corn husks filled with steamed and spiced warm cornmeal. McClard's does serve plain tamales with beans, but the connoisseur's way to get them is as a spread: two big hot tamales on a plate topped with barbecue-sauce–sopped chopped smoked pork shreds, beans, crisp Fritos chips, raw onions, and shredded orange cheese. Reminiscent of Cincinnati five-way chili, a spread is a Mex-Dixie kaleidoscope that is positively addictive.

Layering is a theme in the McClard's kitchen. The menu lists ribs, but it also lists "rib and fry." No special cooking technique here: A plate arrives on which the ribs are completely obscured by a huge heap of French-fried

potatoes. If these were ordinary fries, such a presentation might be annoying, but they are superb: thin and crisp with a lovely burnished complexion. The ribs are hefty ones, their chewy blackened crust painted with eye-opening red sauce that has a vinegar tang. Inside the crust is the most tender, sweet, moist meat, eager to be pulled gently from the bone.

During our last visit to McClard's, we ran into an old *roadfood* friend who was looking mighty svelte—maybe forty pounds lighter than the last time we had seen her, somewhere along the chile road north of El Paso. She fairly skipped over to our table, waving a partially denuded pork rib in the air like a little flag and singing the tidings of her successful new eating program. "Aren't you breaking your diet by eating at McClard's?" we asked her, in this setting filled with vast platters of food that was on no weight-reduction plan we knew about.

"Not at all," she answered. "I'm on the pork plan. All the barbecue I want, and French fries, too. The more ribs I eat, the healthier I feel."

Finally, here was a diet we could relate to!

McClard's Tamale Spread

1 cup chopped onion

2 cloves garlic, minced

2 tablespoons oil

1 pound lean ground chuck or 1 pound cooked, shredded pork shoulder

2 or more cups barbecue sauce of choice

1 teaspoon salt

$1/4$ cup chili powder

1 teaspoon red-pepper flakes

1 teaspoon ground cumin

1 15-ounce can pinto beans, washed and drained

1 bunch green onions, chopped

12 ounces grated cheddar cheese

Fritos, for garnish

1. Sauté onion and garlic in oil in a Dutch oven. If using ground chuck, add it and cook it until well browned, stirring to break up the meat. Drain excess oil. If using shredded pork barbecue, set it aside and continue with recipe.

2. Add all remaining ingredients except beans, green onions, and cheese. Bring to boil, partially cover, and simmer, 30 minutes, stirring occasionally. If mixture gets too dry, add more barbecue sauce to keep it moist. Add beans. *If using pork shoulder, add it now.* Simmer, partially covered, 7 minutes more.

3. Preheat oven to 350°F.

4. Butter a deep 9-by-13-inch baking pan or casserole. Remove tamales from their husks, and put a dense layer of them at the bottom of the casserole pan. Top the tamales with chili, then onions, then cheese.

5. Bake 20 minutes, or until cheese is fully melted and just beginning to brown. Remove from oven and garnish with Fritos.

Makes a 9-by-13-inch pan of tamales; enough to serve 10.

Mike's Donuts

EVERETT, MASSACHUSETTS

*M*ike's Donuts is not a place visited by most visitors to Boston. It is out by the produce market, far off the beaten path; it is a favorite among Beantown cabbies and short-haul truckers. We discovered Mike's while on tour to promote our book *The Encyclopedia of Bad Taste*, when Arlene the Boston cab driver put us in the back of her taxi and took us on a guided tour of all the city's tackiest sites. After a trip up Route 1 towards a Leaning Tower of Pizza restaurant and the humongous Hilltop Steak House (serving more steak to more people than any other place on earth), we went to a tavern with walls decorated by toilet seats as well as its patrons' bounced checks, then Arlene took us around town to look at several hideous crime scenes and murder houses.

As we careened through the produce market, Arlene asked if we were hungry. Of course we were. So, she took us out for donuts, to a place she claimed served Boston's best. Arlene's taxi lurched into Mike's parking lot among a swarm of early morning pickup trucks, police cruisers, delivery vans, and other cabs.

The joint was crowded, noisy, and confusing, its air thick with the aroma of strong coffee, hot pastries, and sugar glaze melting on donuts. The muffins looked mighty good to us, but Arlene would have none of them. Donuts are Mike's specialty, and it was donuts we ate: jelly filled, cinnamon dusted, chocolate frosted, and plain. All were excellent. We especially liked Mike's French crullers—gossamer-twisted circles of eggy batter with a faint sugar crust. Arlene's favorite, the Boston creme donut, was a paradigm of its type, a big, tan, sweet bun loaded with silky cool goo and blanketed on top with a thick sheath of dark chocolate.

When we got home, we worked hard to replicate the donut that we had enjoyed in Boston. It takes some work to make donuts at home, but what a treat they are for a special weekend breakfast, when you feel like going whole hog.

Boston Creme Donuts

DONUTS

1 cup milk

4 tablespoons butter

$1/2$ cup plus $1/2$ teaspoon sugar

$1/2$ teaspoon salt

1 egg

1 package yeast

$1/4$ cup warm water (105–115°F)

$1/2$ teaspoon vanilla

3–$3^1/2$ cups all-purpose flour

Oil, for deep frying

FILLING

1 cup refrigerated, prepared vanilla pudding (we use Swiss Miss)

GLAZE

2 ounces semisweet chocolate

$1/2$ ounce unsweetened chocolate

1 tablespoon butter

1 cup confectioners' sugar

$1/2$ teaspoon vanilla

2–3 tablespoons hot water

1. Make donuts: Scald milk with butter, sugar, and salt, stirring to dissolve sugar. Cool to lukewarm, then beat in egg. Proof yeast in water with $1/2$ teaspoon sugar, until foamy.

2. In a large mixing bowl, combine flour, milk mixture, vanilla, and yeast mixture. Beat until smooth. Add additional flour, if needed, to make a soft dough that pulls from the sides of the bowl.

3. Turn dough onto a floured board and knead, 5 minutes, until smooth. Place in a greased bowl, cover lightly, and let rise in warm place, until double in bulk.

4. Punch down dough, and place on lightly floured surface. Roll to $1/2$-inch thickness. Cut with $2^1/2$-inch biscuit cutter. Place cut pieces 2 inches apart on floured baking sheet, cover lightly, and let rise, 45 minutes, or until nearly doubled.

5. Heat oil in deep fryer or heavy pan to 365°F. Fry donuts, a few at a time, 3 minutes, until golden on one side. Turn with slotted spoon and fry, 2–3 more minutes, on other side. Remove with slotted spoon and drain on paper towels. Cool.

6. Make a small slit in the side of each donut. Fill a pastry bag with the filling. Use a plain tip to push about 2 teaspoons of the filling inside the donut.

7. Make glaze by melting both chocolates with butter in a small, heavy saucepan. Stir in confectioners' sugar and vanilla until smooth. Beat in enough water for easy-spreading consistency. Spread atop each filled donut. Serve immediately, or within a few hours. Any leftovers must be refrigerated, because of the pudding filling.

Makes 18 donuts.

Mt. Cube Farm

ORFORD, NEW HAMPSHIRE

When Meldrim Thomson was Governor of New Hampshire, from 1973 to 1979, he was known for serving pancake breakfasts to legislators and lobbyists at the Governor's Mansion in Concord. The pancakes were made from his wife Gale's batter, and the syrup served with them was New Hampshire maple syrup from the governor's farm in Orford. After his tenure in office, he retired to his beloved farm, where he and his wife continued to serve pancake breakfasts but in this case, to friends and passers-by. Meals were served on paper plates, at card tables arrayed in a dining area not far from the sap evaporators where, in the spring, maple syrup was made.

One spring day, at the height of sugaring season, Governor Thomson took us to the sugar house and showed us a thing or two about the ancient ways of syrup making—how a drop of heavy cream clears the foamy head off the syrup in the evaporator, and how sugarmen traditionally make themselves a lunch snack by dropping a few whole eggs to poach into the boiling, sweet liquid.

Petting Sheba, the old black Labrador retriever who tagged along wherever he went, the governor led us outside to a field of freshly fallen snow and reminisced about sugar-on-snow parties. After the sap has been boiled down, the sugarmen and their families treat themselves to a rare snack around the campfire or stove. They boil the syrup once again, until it thickens, then pour it in a thin stream over clean, packed snow. When the hot syrup hits the cold snow, it stiffens and becomes a taffylike candy known as *frogs* or *leather aprons*. To accompany these sweet treats, sugar makers traditionally serve plain raised donuts and coffee or cider. And, to revive a flagging sweet tooth for more candy, there are always dill pickles on the side!

Sugar on Snow

Clean, freshly fallen show or finely
    crushed ice

1 quart pure maple syrup

12 plain raised donuts

12 sour pickles

Coffee, cider, or hot chocolate

1. If using snow, it must be freshly fallen. Snow can be gathered, packed in pans, and brought indoors, or you can make sugar on snow in the great outdoors. Either way, pack down the clean snow with a clean spatula.

2. In a heavy saucepan over medium heat, cook the maple syrup until it reaches 232°F on a candy thermometer, so that it will form a soft ball when dropped in cold water.

3. Use a tablespoon to drop and drizzle the hot syrup onto the snow, allowing it to splash into patterns. Serve immediately, still in its tray, giving each eater a fork to wind the pieces up off the snow or ice. Accompany the candy with donuts, pickles, and hot beverage of choice.

P.S.: If making sugar on snow with children, be cautions about the hot syrup. It can burn overeager hands and mouths!

Makes 12 servings.

New England Raised Donuts

Raised donuts are ultraplain compared to such sugar-shock modern donuts as Krispy Kreme, but plain is exactly what's required when the point of the donut is to offset the refined sweetness of pure maple syrup. You want something utterly simple that doesn't compete. These donuts are perfect for a sugar-on-snow party; they are also eminently dunkable into coffee or small cups of pure maple syrup.

1 package dry yeast

$^1/_2$ cup plus 1 teaspoon sugar

2 tablespoons tepid water (110°F)

1 egg, beaten

1 cup milk

2 tablespoons butter, melted

$3^1/_2$–$3^3/_4$ cups flour

Oil, for deep frying

1. Combine yeast and 1 teaspoon sugar in the tepid water. Let stand, 5–10 minutes, until foamy.

2. Combine remaining sugar, egg, milk, and melted butter. Add yeast to this mixture, then vigorously combine with $3^{1}/_{2}$ cups of flour to create a smooth, sticky dough. Add a bit more flour if dough is very soft.

3. Place the dough in a buttered bowl, and brush the top of the dough with butter. Cover with a double layer of plastic wrap and let it rise until double in bulk, 2–3 hours.

4. Pound the dough down and, working with half the batch at a time, roll it out on a lightly floured board to a $^{1}/_{2}$-inch thickness. Cut with a $2^{1}/_{2}$–3-inch donut cutter, and put the cut donuts on a lightly floured wooden board. Reroll scraps, and cut them into donuts. Cover donuts loosely with a towel, and allow them to rise another 60 to 90 minutes.

5. Heat oil in deep fryer or large kettle to 375°F. Fry donuts, a few at a time, until brown on one side, turn and fry until evenly browned all over, about 4 minutes total. Remove and drain on paper towels. Serve immediately, while still warm.

Makes 15 donuts and 15 donut holes.

O'Rourke's Diner

O'Rourke's is a silver-sided jewel, tucked among the plebeian storefronts at the north end of Main Street in Middletown, Connecticut. Originally trucked up from the Mountain View diner factory in New Jersey in 1946, it boasts an exterior with gleaming pointed *cowcatcher* corners, a Deco design fillip unique to the Mountain View Company, which went defunct in the mid-1950s. Wrapped in bands of steel with columns of glass brick on both sides of the door, O'Rourke's was expanded once (total seating capacity: forty-five), but it hasn't recently been modernized. It is worn like a fine old saddle—all the more comfortable and inviting for the years of counter culture it exudes. Inside, blue-and-white tiles rim the marble counter; in booths that creak with age, meals are served on unbreakable Hemcoware plates in pale pastel colors; on the counter, near pans of cooling blueberry muffins, newspapers are fanned out for patrons to read. Each booth has its own jukebox, but the prominent sounds are those of conversation among patrons, waitresses, and cook.

"He looks older to me," says one seasoned customer, sipping coffee and watching another regular walk out the door.

"He's a cop," notes Barbara Feegel, head waitress for more than a decade. "All cops look old."

The clientele of O'Rourke's is an agreeable combination of old-timers, students and faculty from nearby Wesleyan University, well-dressed local professionals, and a smattering of not-so-well-dressed nonprofessionals, too. Some patrons, like Wesleyan professor J. Seeley, are such steady customers that they have a table or counterstool that every other regular recognizes as theirs, and they may even have a unique dish named for them. (The J. Seeley Special is an omelet filled with onions, tomatoes, guacamole, and cheese, so named because Seeley is a southwestern food aficionado, and showed the chef how to make guacamole.) A few veterans have been around long enough to remember and even use such diner anachronisms as *trilby* (any sandwich with onions added), *Coney Island chicken* (a hot dog), and *dog soup* (a glass of water). Proprietor Brian O'Rourke grew up in the diner, which his uncle John established. Brian began as a potato peeler in 1958, when he was seven. He arrives each morning at three to start breakfast, and is a fanatic about this place of his—about its history and about its current status as a preeminent bastion of diner cooking, both classic and modern.

Brian loves to talk about the food he makes. He can regale you with a short thesis about something as simple as large-quantity bread baking (his repertoire includes Norwegian rye, Portuguese sweet bread, potato bread, pain noir, banana bread, and muffins) and he delights in enumerating the complexities of his deluxe Sunday breakfast, which includes seasonal omelets (spring grass; November turkey; and a July combo of salmon, asparagus, and Swiss cheese), southern-style biscuits and gravy, and Irish soda-bread pancakes topped with cream, sabayon, and fruit. On a May afternoon a few years back, he enthralled us with a clever story about how he offered free meals to a local fisherman to get fresh shad and shad roe for his dinner menu. One weekend last fall, his spaghetti dinner featured a nine-variety-wild-mushroom-and-wine sauce, because he was able to barter breakfasts for mushrooms with the local mushroom man. Recently, he explained in mouth-watering detail how he made an all-greens soup because he came across a good supply of fresh collard and mustard greens, and the caraway in his garden was ripe for picking; these were combined with kale, sorrel, and ricotta, sour cream, and yogurt to create a thick, invigorating brew.

If you are a regular customer, or even if you are a stranger and express interest in the food, it is likely you will be given something to taste. Brian O'Rourke is an inveterate experimenter who almost always is working on some new dish—roasted eggplant soup, broccoli pesto, pumpkin-oatmeal pancakes—and he relishes trying out innovations on customers. J. Seeley, who has been coming to the diner for more than twenty years, recalls his first visit after Brian bought the place from his uncle John, long ago. "It was a rainy day and I was sitting on a stool between two cans that were collecting water leaking from the roof. I ordered split-pea soup, and on the side he brought me a little plate with crackers on it. Of all things—*homemade* crackers, topped with melted cheese. I knew something good was about to happen to this old diner. I became a regular, and now I eat lunch here four or five times a week. I never order anything, though. I just sit down and something experimental gets put in front of me. I love Brian's soups, stews, and shepherd's pies. Of course, I have to taste the J. Seeley omelet periodically,

just to check. I was worried at first it might taste a little too *California*, but it's a good combination." Whenever J. visits New Mexico, he brings back bushels of chili peppers for Brian to roast or to dry.

"I've been doing a lot of drying lately," Brian told us one September, holding up an old plastic quart carton that once contained ricotta, but now held chili powder made from hundreds of dried, ground, golden cayenne peppers. "Here, smell," he said, opening the top. The aroma was dizzying—sharp, earthy, sunny. "This is a season's worth," he said. "All I need is a pinch for my soups or sauces." Then, even though we had just finished dessert, he brought out a little crock of chili, so we could taste. Brian watched as we spooned into it and he beamed when we polished off the little bowl. Clearly, this is a man who loves his work. And, let us say after having eaten at O'Rourke's on and off for the last twenty years: What's not to love?

Have a good sniff when you enter. If you are a student of dinerology, or if you are in the slightest bit hungry, you are bound to swoon with pleasure. In the morning, the air is perfumed with the aroma of frying spuds laced with onions, and bacon sizzling on the grill; later in the day the fragrance is more that of hot meatloaf and plates piled high with mashed potatoes with gravy cascading down the fluffy white mountain-sides; of split pea soup or bluefish chowder wafting its bouquet of spice into the air as it is whisked to a hungry customer, and of creamy ched-dar cheese melting in the old-fashioned steam box.

The cheese is being melted, most likely, for a steamed cheeseburger, here referred to as a *steamer*. O'Rourke's is known for its steamers, as are about a half dozen other restaurants in central Connecticut; in fact, it was at Jack's Lunch (now defunct), also on Main Street in Middle-town, that the first steamer was served. Jack Fitzgerald started in the food business early in the twentieth century, with a lunch wagon fea-turing all kinds of steamed meals, which he sold to local factory work-ers. When he opened his little café in the 1920s, steamed food was con-sidered especially healthful by nutrition-conscious people who were starting to worry that anything fried was difficult to digest. Popular as Jack's steamed-beef-and-cheese sandwiches were on Main Street, how-ever, they never went the path of nationally famous Buffalo chicken wings or Chicago deep-dish pizza or Tucson chimichangas. The steamed cheeseburger remained a localized Connecticut obsession, cooked by steam heat in a small metal steam box made in state espe-cially for the job.

Both hamburger *and* cheese are cooked in the steam box, each in its own separate tray. The extraordinarily juicy beef patty is topped with the oozing blob of melted cheddar, then set forth upon a fluff-cen-tered hard roll and garnished with a thick slice off a crisp, raw onion and a schmear of mustard. It is possible to order a steamer with lettuce or mayonnaise, or without the onion and mustard but, in the diners of central Connecticut, any of these other configurations are considered as serious a *faux pas* as asking a waiter at the Russian Tea Room for a bubble-pack of corn syrup to accompany your blini and beluga caviar.

The key to a steamer's goodness is the cheese. Moderately aged cheddar is best; when steamed, it transforms into a lush, pearlescent mass that is just viscous enough to seep into every crevice of the meat below, but not so runny that it escapes the sandwich. (Although it *will* seriously leak grease, so caution, balance, and many napkins are required.) In fact, this cheese is so beloved by O'Rourke's regulars that many people order it on things other than hamburgers. Hot dogs and slabs of meatloaf and plates of fried potatoes get topped with steamed cheese; some prefer steamed cheese alone in a roll; and the connoisseur's choice is hot apple pie covered with a thick mantle of it—a perfect combo and the epitome of deluxe diner dessert.

How to Steam Cheese

You don't have to be a do-it-yourself type to rig your own steam box at home. Using Brian O'Rourke's expert advice, we jury-rigged one using a large skillet, a metal colander with feet, a big heatproof bowl, and a clean, empty 6½-ounce tuna can.

Here's how: Put about one inch of water in the skillet and place on the stove over medium heat. Place the colander above the water. Put 4–6 ounces of cheddar cheese in the tuna can and, when the water begins to boil, put the tuna can in the colander. Then, cover the colander with the big heatproof bowl, trapping the steam inside. In only a matter of minutes, the cheese will melt, then all you have to do is use a spoon to scoop it out onto a hamburger, a hard roll, or a piece of apple pie.

Makes enough cheese for 3–4 servings.

P.S. It is actually possible to cook the hamburger in the makeshift steam box if you want to be a classicist about your steamer. Put a half-inch patty of lean raw ground beef in another tuna can and steam both burger and cheese at the same time.

O'Rourke's Roasted Tomato Soup

10 ripe plum tomatoes

5 tablespoons olive oil

2 garlic cloves, minced

1/2 teaspoon dried oregano, crumbled

1/4 teaspoon dried basil, crumbled

1/2 teaspoon black pepper

1/2 cup finely chopped onion

1 cup chicken broth

1/4 cup red Burgundy wine

1/2 cup ricotta

1/2 cup heavy cream

1/2 cup tomato paste

2 tablespoons freshly grated Parmesan

Spinach pesto, for garnish
(recipe follows)

1. Preheat oven to 475°F.

2. Cut the tomatoes in half lengthwise and lay cut-side down in a jelly-roll pan. Brush generously with 3 tablespoons oil, and sprinkle with garlic, oregano, basil, and pepper. Roast tomatoes until edges are charred, about 20 minutes.

3. Scrape tomatoes, oil, and herbs from pan into food processor. Process briefly, until not quite smooth.

4. In a saucepan, cook the onion in the remaining 2 tablespoons oil until it is soft. Whisk in the tomato puree, broth, and wine. Then whisk in ricotta, cream, and tomato paste. Finally, stir in Parmesan. Add pepper, basil, and oregano to taste. Bring soup to simmer. Add a dollop of spinach pesto to each serving.

Makes 5 cups.

Spinach Pesto for Roasted Tomato Soup

1 10-ounce bunch spinach, thoroughly washed and drained, stems discarded

1/4 teaspoon salt

2 garlic cloves

1 tablespoon butter

1 cup pine nuts

1 cup freshly grated Parmesan

1 cup olive oil

In a food processor, puree spinach, salt, garlic, butter, pine nuts, and Parmesan, until smooth. Gradually blend in oil.

Makes 3 cups.

Porubsky's Grocery

TOPEKA, KANSAS

Charlie Porubsky, born and raised in the Little Russia community of North Topeka, Kansas, came home after World War II. Shortly thereafter, when the old corner grocery by the train tracks on North East Sardou—the only retail store in a neighborhood of modest private homes—came up for sale, he and his mother Katherine bought it. Although it was on the wrong side of the tracks, far from Topeka's shopping district, business was good, because Sardou was a thoroughfare. In addition to neighbors who stopped in weekly for staples and daily for cold-cut sandwiches, Porubsky's attracted a healthy drive-by trade. In 1951, when they paid off the mortgage, Charlie and his mother thought they had it made. But then came the great flood of '51. As Charlie puts it, "The whole damn business washed away."

Although severely damaged, the little store was rebuilt, but an ominous thing happened in the wake of the natural disaster: A floodproof bridge was constructed just north of Little Russia. The main artery that brought motorists past the Porubskys' front door was turned into a dead-end street, and rendered virtually obsolete. Traffic stopped. Charlie watched his dream disappear.

One cold day in autumn, a local businessman named George Walls found his way to the deserted grocery store looking for a bologna sandwich. Charlie's mother was at a stove behind the meat counter stirring a pot of chili for her children to have for lunch. "My mother could cook anything," Charlie now boasts.

"Say, that sure smells good," Mr. Walls noted as he waited for his sandwich. "Do you think you could make some for me?" Mrs. Porubsky gave him a bowlful to eat. He enjoyed it so much that he asked if she could make more the next day for the other boys at his office to have at lunch time. She did, they liked it, and soon the word began to spread.

More Topekans started coming to the store to ask for servings of the delicious ground-beef and bean stew. It was tasty, cheap, and quick; it was a fine antidote to the cold Kansas winter. For those who discovered the joy of Porubsky's chili, the little neighborhood store no longer seemed so far out of the way. Bypassed by urban planning and on a road to nowhere, it became a destination for blue-collar and white-collar workers on their lunch hours, for politicians eager to meet and greet ordinary citizens in the state's capitol, and even for passing trainmen with fifteen minutes to spare. Charlie learned from his mother how to make the celebrated dish, and his son and grandsons have since learned from him. Today, Porubsky's Grocery is known throughout the state; its chili is a cherished culinary attraction between Kansas City and the Plains.

Still, it's something of a rarity. You can get it only for lunch, 11 AM to 2 PM, Monday through Thursday. The Porubsky family likes to keep the narrow aisles of the shop clear on Friday and Saturday, so inventory can be restocked and neighborhood people can do their grocery shopping. Any day chili is on the menu, the homey store gets so mobbed with people waiting to eat that there is no room for shoppers to navigate among the shelves.

It is strictly a seasonal meal, available October through March. Charlie observes, "The colder the weather, the more chili we sell. On a very cold day, we'll go through more than fifty gallons." On a blustery Monday late in November, we saw two men from a road crew sitting at the bar ordering bowl after bowl to brace themselves for a windswept afternoon on the prairie.

Some people have twisted Charlie's arm in hopes of getting him to make big batches for parties or to package it for sending through the mail, and some have waltzed in the door and tried to order twenty-five gallons at a time. All such supplications are met by irrefutable logic: If Charlie sold his chili in large quantities, there wouldn't be enough for the customers who come to the store for lunch. Supplies are further limited by the fact that it is all cooked on a single four-burner apartment stove just behind the butcher counter. "It works like a champ!" announces Charlie's son, Charlie, Jr., who takes a moment away from alternately stirring two pots of beans and two of spiced meat to pat the white enamel sides of the old appliance with the affection a hunter shows toward a loyal dog.

As it is ladled from the stove, it is a soupy kind of chili, about equal amounts of beans and coarse-ground beef in a rich, cinnabar emulsion with a nice harmony of spices. Each serving, presented in a disposable bowl, is accompanied by two cellophane-wrapped packets of Lance saltines, which are essential: Crumble them into the chili and they thicken it, as well as adding a welcome note of starchy flavor. On the side comes a tiny paper cup with shredded raw onion for sprinkling on top.

The majority of Porubsky customers get their chili with a *plate*, which is a small platter of square lunch-meat slices and cheese slices, each cut into two rectangles and neatly fanned out with two pieces of white bread and two of whole wheat, also bisected so the cold cuts will fit perfectly into half sandwiches. Spicy German mustard is supplied in squeeze bottles.

Garnishing every plate are pickles, which have become nearly as famous as the chili. They are briny dills that the Porubsky family buys whole, then doctors. "Mom and Aunt Pat cut them," Charlie, Jr., says. "Then, we add the spices to give them a bite, so they hit your nose like a shot of horseradish." The peppery pickle chunks make eyes water and lips tingle. Although they are fine for popping in the mouth with a cold-cut sandwich, the connoisseur's way with Porubsky pickles is to toss a handful directly into a bowl of chili, adding a strange, puckery kind of fire to the brew. Customers who like their lunch *really* hot grab a couple of raw jalapeño peppers on their way in the door from a cardboard box that Charlie, Sr., often keeps near the cash register.

The beverage most locals get to accompany their chili and plates is sweet carbonated soda, known hereabouts as *pop*. Beer is available, but it is not too popular. Charlie Porubsky explains: "Unlike Kansas City, employers in Topeka kinda frown on beer for lunch."

Lydia Porubsky, Charlie's wife, then told us why coffee is no longer available. "We had to stop serving it. The women would eat a bowl of chili, then sit and sip their coffee, sit and sip, while men were standing outside waiting to come in for lunch." No one lingers more than thirty minutes for a meal in this busy place; it is only polite to eat fast, then vacate your seat so someone else can get a chance to eat. The maximum capacity of Porubsky's dining room is thirty-six people.

The Porubskys have lunch service down to a simple science. When you find a seat in the dining room, Lydia or some other family member takes your order. The most popular configuration for a pair of normal appetites dining together is two bowls of chili and one cold-cut plate to split. When you order, you must say if you want all hot pickles (other-

wise you also get a few ordinary dills) or an extra bowl of hot pickles for throwing in your chili (you do!). Lydia calls your order through the doorway from the dining room to whomever is working behind the butcher counter, where the chili is made and the plates are kept. Within a minute, the meal is put on a tray and brought to a small pedestal in the doorway, where Lydia picks it up and brings it to the table.

When you are finished eating, you get up and stroll out through the grocery. There, at the cash register, is Charlie, Sr., a big, bright-eyed gent in a paper butcher's cap who enjoys jawboning with his regular customers, as well as meeting new ones from around the country. Charlie never ceases to be amazed that people from all fifty states come to track down the little grocery store that has become a Kansas legend. Tell him what you ate and he computes the bill—$1.95 for a bowl of chili, $1.95 for a plate of cold cuts, plus the cost of pop—and he rings it up on a well-worn cash register that was included with the business when he and his mother bought it fifty-one years ago.

Porubsky Chili

Porubsky's Grocery serves chili midwestern style, meaning the beef is ground, beans are included, and the spice level is low. Not one of the Porubsky family was able to write down the recipe, for the simple reason that there is no recipe. It is an uncomplicated dish made by taste, feel, and experience: a little of this, a jot of that, a dash more of something else. We spent a morning watching Charlie, Jr., prepare a day's worth, so here is our educated-guess version of Porubsky's pride. Its heat level can be adjusted by using hot or mild chili powder, and by adding more or less hot sauce.

1 cup chopped onion

2 cloves garlic, minced

2 tablespoons vegetable oil

2 pounds coarsely ground beef chuck

1½ teaspoons salt

3 tablespoons chili powder

1 tablespoon ground cumin

2 teaspoons Worcestershire sauce

1 tablespoon sugar

3 cups tomato sauce

2 cups water

2 16-ounce cans red kidney beans, drained

Tabasco sauce, to taste (10 drops lends a faint heat.)

Saltine crackers, for serving

Dill pickles, thickly sliced and halved to produce bite-sized nuggets, for garnish

1. In a heavy saucepan, sauté onions and garlic in oil over medium heat, until soft. Add beef and salt. Cook until beef is browned throughout, breaking it up with a fork as it cooks. Drain any excess fat.

2. Add chili powder, cumin, Worcestershire sauce, sugar, tomato sauce, and water. Bring to a low boil and simmer, 30 minutes stirring occasionally.

3. Add the beans and simmer, 15 minutes more. Add Tabasco sauce and more salt, to taste.

4. Serve with Saltines crumbled on top of each portion, and dill-pickle pieces as a garnish.

Makes 6 servings.

Horseradish Pickles

1 32-ounce jar kosher dill-pickle
    halves (about four large pickles),
    with brine

$^1/_2$ cup prepared horseradish

1 teaspoon ground cayenne pepper

Pour brine from the pickle jar into a large bowl. Mix the horseradish and cayenne pepper into the brine. Cut the pickles into large bite-sized pieces and reimmerse them in the brine. Cover and refrigerate several hours, or overnight.

Makes 20 servings.

Ranchman's Café

PONDER, TEXAS

*I*n a sleepy encampment by the train tracks, at the northern fringe of the Dallas/Fort Worth metroplex, Ranchman's Café—known among fans as the Ponder Steak House—is the sort of red-meat haven you'll find only in the Lone Star State. "Welcome to Texas!" chimed one well-fed good ol' boy at us, as he pushed his way out the creaky swinging door, looking like he just sold his prize bull for a million dollars. Handing his denuded T-bone to the hound that had faithfully gazed in at him through the storefront window as he dined, he strolled along the dusty Ponder main street enjoying a smoke. The dog settled in on the raised sidewalk to savor his bone.

Ponder serves cowboy-style steaks on rickety, unclothed tables. The meat is hand cut and platter-sized, sizzled on a hot griddle until it develops a wickedly tasty crust. Although tender, these steaks are not the silver butterknife cuts of expense-account dining rooms; they are of substantial density that requires a sharp knife and rewards a good chew with tides of flavor. Hand-cut French fries come on the side, but if you call the café an hour and a half ahead of your arrival, they'll put a baked potato in the oven and have it ready by the time you sit down to eat that steak. After all that time in the oven, the white insides of the potatoes are as tender as cream, and sheer joy to push through the puddles of steak juice that flow from the meat as you cut it.

As we forked up our flawless meal, a couple of uniformed Texas Rangers occupied the booth next to ours, and no sooner had they ordered steaks than their two-way radio called them out on an emergency. "Keep it cooking," they told the chef behind the counter as they charged out the door, jumped in their cruiser, and sped away. Not ten minutes later, they returned, without having broken a sweat.

"Did you get your man?" the waitress asked, setting their steaming hot steak-and-potato meals down before them.

"We always get our man," one ranger answered as he twirled his steak knife off the table with a gunslinger's flourish and prepared to cut.

Perfect Baked Potato

There are no tricks to cooking a great baked potato; there is just time . . . and plenty of it. You need to start with a potato that has a high starch content, such as a russet. Wash and scrub the exterior and pat it dry. Do not pierce it or poke it with nails designed to make the inside bake faster. Allow one good-sized potato per person.

Heat the oven to 350°F. Place the potatoes on a middle rack, close the door, and wait 90–120 minutes. When the potatoes are done, the outside will be leathery and still pliable. (If you cook the potatoes too long, the outside will become brittle.) The inside should feel soft through the skin.

Remove the potatoes from oven, and when ready to serve (while still hot!), slice each potato lengthwise and fill each half with butter and/or sour cream or, if you're on a diet, lemon juice and pepper.

Ratner's Dairy Restaurant

NEW YORK, NEW YORK

*E*ven if he approaches your table from behind, you will know Harry the waiter is on his way by the weary shuffle of his feet and the sighs he utters as he goes about his job, serving platters of smoked fish and bowls of matzoh ball soup. He is a good waiter, even speedy, belying his languid demeanor, but part of his job here at Ratner's on Delancy Street is to let you, the customer, know that the world is a sorrowful place indeed—a task he performs with every fiber of his being. There is a method to this melancholy: with life so sad, the Jewish comfort food Harry serves is all the more needed, and all the tastier.

"Been here long?" we ask him as the meal concludes with hunks of babka and coffee.

"Oh, not long," he manages to utter.

"Really? You seem like a veteran, you know the score," we say to butter him up. We then realize that even this friendly interjection has interrupted the slow unfolding of his delivery. He goes back to the beginning:

"Oh, not long . . . just thirty-two years."

Not every waiter in this nonagenarian institution is a veteran. As we spoon into our flamingo-pink borscht one winter's afternoon, Harry and another senior colleague take young Jeff, a new boy, under their wing, and point him to a table of customers.

"They're yours," says Harry. "Go to them."

Harry's peer speaks up in a thick Eastern European accent. "You take care of them and we will watch. We will give you a waiter's clinic."

"A cleaning?" says Jeff, mishearing the accented caption to the scene. He is scared to death of working under these watchful experts' eyes. And sure enough, when Jeff sets down the plate of delicious baked-together onion rolls that every table gets along with pats of sweet butter, Harry strolls along nearly in his shadow, rotating the plate ninety degrees to fit

Harry's well-honed vision of precisely how a table should be arranged. And so it goes: The waiter's clinic Jeff endures with Harry and his co-worker is a meal's worth of entertainment, and would command all our attention if the food itself weren't so remarkable.

Ratner's is Kosher, known to observant Jews as a *dairy restaurant*, meaning that its kitchen is supervised by a Rabbi and serves no meat. There are fish of all kinds: broiled, smoked, pickled, kippered, fried, as well as tuna by the can and classical gefilte fish served either warm or cold. There are crunchy potato pancakes (*latkes*) served with homemade apple sauce or sour cream. The sour cream, which also comes with the excellent blintzes (available filled with cheese, potato, *kasha* [buckwheat groats], or different fruits), is actually *soured* cream—a great ivory mound of clotted cream with a few honest lumps, thick enough to stand a spoon in.

One day at lunch, we are seated next to a twenty-something gentle-man with a heavy Russian accent who apparently is new to America . . . but dead set on not being taken for a fool. When Harry sets his block of baked-together onion rolls before him, the greenhorn says in his best English, "Please, take these away. Bring me fresh!"

At this, Harry leans on the table with one hand, so tormented by the request he can barely stand up any more. "You want fresh?" he says in disbelief that someone doubts Ratner's kitchen.

"Please!" the young man says as politely as he can.

Oy! Without a word, Harry swoops the rolls off the table, shuffles back toward the kitchen, and returns with what appear to us to be the exact same rolls he just took away. (For the record, never in our Ratner's experience have the dinner rolls been less than impeccably fresh.) He sets them down triumphantly.

"Aha!" says the new boy, tearing one away from the block with great joy. "This is fresh! Now, bring me kasha varnishkes and I will tell my mother I have eaten well."

In 2000, Ratner's changed dramatically, folding the dairy restaurant into a retro club called Lansky Lounge. Robert Harmatz, grandson of founder Jacob Harmatz, explained, "The younger people moving into the neighborhood don't really care for the heavy kind of food we've always served." Kosher food is no longer available, and the old-time waiters are gone. Thus, the preceding vignette, which we wrote in the last days of the twentieth century, has become culinary history.

Matzoh Brei

Pronounced "matsa brî," this is Jewish comfort food, generally served at breakfast or brunch, but also wonderful as a quickly made late-night snack. Ratner's recipe for two people calls for three matzohs, which we don't believe is nearly enough to split. We've increased the measure of ingredients accordingly, added sour cream, and also upped the amount of butter used. It is impossible to use too much butter when making matzoh brei.

6–8 whole matzohs (egg-onion matzohs are good, too)	$1/4$ teaspoon white pepper
4 eggs	Sour cream and/or apple sauce, for serving
1 teaspoon salt	6 tablespoons butter

1. Crush matzohs very coarsely in a large bowl. Do not crumble. Pieces should be about the size of playing cards. Fill the bowl with water, and *immediately* drain off all the water. You want the matzoh pieces damp but not totally soaked.

2. Stir in eggs, salt, and pepper, crushing the matzoh a bit more as you stir, so that you get a variety of pieces from crumbles to matchbook size.

3. Melt 4 tablespoons butter in a heavy skillet over medium-high heat. Add the matzoh mixture and gently flatten it out in the pan with a spatula. Dot the top of the mixture with the remaining butter. When underside is golden brown, flip the large pancake. It's okay if it breaks up as you flip it; in fact, we believe in breaking it up and stirring the semicooked matzoh around in the pan (with more butter, of course). When it is mostly browned, it is ready to serve.

4. Serve hot with sour cream and/or apple sauce.

Makes 4 servings.

Roque's Carnitas Wagon

SANTA FE, NEW MEXICO

Roque Garcia and his partner Mona Cavalli station their chuckwagon at the edge of Santa Fe's Plaza, just around the corner from the Portale of the Place of the Governors, just before lunch time almost every day but Tuesdays between Easter and Halloween, and sometimes until Thanksgiving. Dining at Roque's is strictly informal. There are no white-clothed tables, no slick young waitstaff, no wine list, and no celebrity chef cleverly reinventing southwestern cuisine. Pay Mona three dollars, plus the cost of your lemonade or soda, then find a place to feast on a simple pleasure that no pretense could improve.

What you get is a sandwich folded inside a large, sturdy, flour tortilla that has been heated on a grate over a charcoal fire. Inside is meat, plenty of it—top round thinly sliced and seasoned in a garlic-and-soy-sauce marinade. At the wagon, piles of this sopped beef are cooked on a grate over a hot, open fire with sliced yellow onions and green chilies (New Mexican chilies when they are in season, in the fall, Anaheims the rest of the year). The melange is tossed vigorously with tongs over the fire, as the meat chars along its edges, engulfed in smoke, and the onions and peppers turn limp. Nearly a half-pound of it is piled into the tortilla and topped with a salsa made from tomatoes, onions, and chopped jalapeño peppers. The hefty sandwich is tightly wrapped in foil so it can be carried without serious spillage.

It is a jolly mess. As soon as you peel back the foil and try to gather up the tortilla for eating, chunks of salsa tumble out, meat juice leaks, onions slither, and plump circles of earth-green chili pepper pop free. There is a tall garbage can near the carnitas wagon, and it is not unusual to see two or three well-dressed customers gathered around it, bending over at the waist and chomping on their sandwiches so that all their spillage falls right into the trash. The choice location for eating, though, is on the plaza itself, on a bench. Here you can sit and lean far forward as you dine, thus sparing your shirt and lap, and providing resident pigeons the carnitas banquet to which they are now accustomed.

"We are *New* Mexican, not Mexican," Mona explains. "That is why we use beef, rather than pork." The beef, which spends only enough time over the hot fire to absorb a whiff of smoke flavor, glistens with moisture. It is tenderly toothsome, with a lush meat-and-marinade smack, which could have no better accent than the taste of fresh, fleshy New Mexican peppers. The whole affair, cushioned by its big circle of warm, wheaty tortilla, is a taste experience that is fundamentally and deliciously southwestern.

Roque is a native New Mexican, born and raised in Santa Fe, and so familiar with local ways, he boasts, "I can see someone and tell you if they are from Santa Fe, Española (twenty miles north), or Las Vegas (forty miles east), just by the way they walk and dress. Españolans wear lighter colors, cowboy shirts—real ones, not fancy, and Wranglers. In Las Vegas, they are more patient, more calm. Santa Feans are faster, they move quickly, their clothes are bright. After all, we are becoming a big city."

Santa Fe was not yet a big city when Roque, now in his midfifties, grew up near the plaza, but its culture has always been a lush one, and it has long been known for its exotic food. Roque well remembers how many street vendors there used to be around town—people hawking tamales, hard-boiled eggs, taquitos, even pickled pigs-feet from jars. They sold them from carts and walked from bar to bar, offering them to hungry patrons.

Those memories inspired his carnitas wagon. Ten years ago, after the fall chile harvest, Roque and three of his buddies were sitting around drinking beer and roasting peppers. They got hungry. Roque went to the refrigerator and found a roast. Recalling a meat-and-chili meal his mother, Conferina Garcia de Salmeron, used to make for him and his eleven brothers and sisters, he cut up the roast, cooked it with peppers, and served it in flour tortillas. "If you have garlic and oregano, you can do almost anything," says Roque, who has been in the restaurant trade most of his life. His pals liked what he served so much that they decided to make it a business and sell sandwiches of *carnitas*, which means "little meats," from a wagon on the plaza.

The plan was that Roque would make carnitas, and another of the partners, John Coventry, would make what are known as hand pies—a kind of Southwestern croque monsieur of ham and cheese between bread cooked in a mold over an open fire. But there was a big problem: In the mid-1980s, there were no clear laws about food vending in Santa Fe. Almost as soon as Roque opened up, the health department demanded: *Where is the washroom?* Roque pondered the question, and answered with

signed letters from the officer of a nearby bank and from a bigwig at the museum on the plaza saying that Roque's staff (he and Mona) were allowed to use their restrooms. That got Roque a reprieve, and he soon bought out his partners and eliminated the hand pies, which weren't selling nearly as well as the carnitas. However, as Santa Fe grew and more vendors moved onto the plaza, the situation grew ugly. "They were crazy years," Roque recalls about the now-infamous food-vendor wars, when fights broke out over who could park where. Roque himself managed to avoid becoming a casualty, he says, only because he hadn't yet arrived on the day when the big battle (between Speedy Fred and the hot dog man) broke out and made front-page news in the local paper.

At the end of the decade, peace was established when the city had vendors draw lots for location. Roque drew what was considered the worst spot—not even on the plaza, but around the corner, to the north-east, on Washington Street. No vendor had ever set up there, because no one wanted to be away from so much pedestrian traffic. And, besides, smoke from Roque's charcoal grill set off the fire alarm in the nearby Museum of Fine Arts. However, that smoke—which smells of sizzling beef and onions and peppers—also turned out to be Roque's secret weapon. When the wind is blowing right, you can smell carnitas halfway across the plaza, and so, even those who might not see the wagon, are drawn to it by the tantalizing smell.

As much as the carnitas wagon attracts strolling tourists, at least half the lunch crowd each day are locals. In the spring, around Easter time, in the first week after Roque and Mona have returned from their winter vacation, cars cruise past on Washington Street tooting their horns to welcome them back. For many Santa Feans, the charm of Roque's—beyond its tasty food—is its simplicity. The carnitas wagon is a reminder of an older Santa Fe before the city was quite so chic, when the plaza was less a magnet for visitors and more a town square where citizens came to shop, meet, and play. "People really used the plaza back then," Roque reminisces about his youth. "There were grocery stores, shoe stores, drug stores. This was the place where all of Santa Fe felt at home. The plaza was filled with pigeons and children chasing pigeons."

Carnitas

Carnitas taste best when the meat and peppers are cooked over an open charcoal fire, but it is possible to prepare them in a hot skillet.

2 tablespoons oregano

4 cloves garlic, minced

1/4 cup soy sauce

1/4 cup vegetable oil

1/4 cup beer

1 1/2 pounds top round or sirloin sliced into 1/4-inch strips against the grain

1 large yellow onion, sliced thin

5 fresh green chiles, sliced in circles, with seeds (New Mexican peppers preferred; Anaheims are acceptable)

4 broad flour tortillas, warmed

Salsa (recipe follows)

1. Combine oregano, garlic, soy sauce, oil, and beer. Marinate beef a minimum of 12 hours, preferably 24 hours. Drain and discard marinade.

2. On a screen over an open fire, or in a hot, greased skillet, cook meat, onion, and peppers, about 5 minutes, tossing almost constantly, until meat is well browned.

3. Use tongs to lift a heap of the meat mixture from the grate or skillet, allowing any excess juice to drip away, and place $1/4$ of the mixture into a warm flour tortilla. Top with salsa (recipe follows), fold the tortilla over, and bunch up some aluminum foil around it. Serve immediately.

Makes 4 servings.

Carnitas Salsa

2 cups diced fresh tomatoes

2 cloves garlic, minced

2–6 jalapeño peppers, finely chopped,
    to taste

1 small onion, chopped

2 tablespoons fresh cilantro, chopped
    (optional)

Combine all ingredients. Chill until ready to serve.

Makes 2$1/2$ cups.

Roseland Apizza

Roseland is officially named Roseland Apizza, the *A* added to the beginning of *pizza* to express a Neapolitan flavor in the way in which the word is said, which is actually more like "uh-*beets*." Although its interior has been recently remodeled, the outside is vintage neighborhood Italian-Americana, with two separate entrances, a side door for the take-out window, and a front door for the dining room.

It was originally a bread bakery, opened in 1935, and known prior to World War II for delivering sturdy Italian bread loaves direct to customers throughout the Naugatuck Valley. Proprietor John Scatolini charged homemakers ten cents for a large loaf, a nickel for a small. When wartime gas rationing made home delivery unfeasible, Mr. Scatolini's baker, who had come from Italy with recipes then little known in the U.S., had a novel idea. "Why don't we use the bread ovens to make pizza?" he said.

A single booth was installed in the shop, and John's thirteen-year-old daughter Lina drew a large, detailed picture of a pizza to show what one looked like to customers unfamiliar with the dish. "I explained to people who came in what it was, and how good it tasted," recalls Lina, who grew up in the kitchen and is now omnipresent in the little restaurant run by her sons. "It is, simply, a tomato pie. A round of dough is rolled out flat and spread with crushed plum tomatoes, anchovies, and a little grated cheese, then baked in the bread oven. Mozzarella was always an option."

Some old timers still come to eat plain tomato pie; others get the long-time favorite "Roseland Special," a pie topped with mozzarella, mushrooms, and sausage. "We make the pork sausage," Lina says, explaining with equanimity that "You cannot buy good sausage. You must grind it yourself from good pork butts." Roseland's homemade sausage is toothsome, succulent meat, lightly seasoned and strewn across the pies in rugged clumps that sing sweet harmony with spinach or broccoli, cheese, and sauce.

The crust of the pizza is what connoisseurs know as New Haven style. "I make a dough that isn't so elastic," explains Gary, Lina's son, who likes to carry on a conversation while gently swirling his everpresent glass of red wine—on special days, it is a rugged Cabernet that he makes himself, using an old wine press. "I could throw my dough in the air maybe once or twice, but we're too busy to spin and twirl in this kitchen. We pound it down and use a rolling pin." The result is a cooked crust that is thin but not quite brittle, with enough brawn to support all but the weightiest combinations of ingredients and to allay the pizza-eater's primal fears: slice collapse and topping slippage.

Gary uses two ovens to cook pizzas, one that runs hot, for those made with the sturdy meats and vegetables typical of pizzeria menus; the other slower, for white pizzas topped with fragile seafood. Roseland makes some spectacularly lavish pies, such as a lobster, shrimp, and scallop pizza drizzled with butter, and a shrimp casino pie with bacon, mozzarella, fresh garlic, and countless jumbo shrimp. For us, the one must-eat specialty is the relatively uncomplicated Connecticut classic, white clam pizza: no mozzarella, no tomato sauce, just a crowd of freshly shucked Rhode Island clams strewn across a crust frosted with olive oil and scattered with bits of basil, parsley, and oregano (all from Lina's garden), thin sliced garlic, a twist of cracked black pepper, and a scattering of grated Parmigiano Reggiano. The nectar of the whole clams insinuates itself into the surface of the crust, giving every crunch exhilarating marine zest.

"Cooking is like music," Gary says in response to our verbal rhapsodies one evening, after plowing through a white clam pie at a booth near the kitchen. "You have to feel it in here . . ."—he knocks a fist to his chest—"And when you roll the dough, the music is in your hands." Struck with inspiration, he sets his wine glass down, goes back to the kitchen and returns with both hands tightly holding a package wrapped with white butcher paper close to his waist. Like a spy about to deliver a secret weapon, he peels back the paper to reveal a straw-yellow hunk of Parmesan cheese, holding it out from his side for us to admire. Its aroma is powerful, even in this dining room that is *always* perfumed by the wheaty smell of hot crust coming from the ovens. His thumb lovingly caresses the block of mature cheese to show how fine and delicate its surface is—ready to grate smoothly or be split into slim leaves. He is beaming; no words are needed to express his admiration for this excellent ingredient.

The baker's oven is only part of Roseland's distinction. "The first thing I was taught as a little girl was to make pasta," Gary's mother Lina remembers. "My father had a stool for me to stand on so I could reach the table." In the 1950s, Lina added ravioli and spaghetti to the menu; now, along with her old friend Josephine, she hand cuts Roseland's ravioli, which are filled with cheese, meat, spinach, or lobster, and also makes wide ribbons of dough for glorious lasagna. Pasta dough is made

in a big mixer used since World War II and, although Lina still likes to turn the crank of the pasta machine by hand—"you have more control, better feel"—Gary is thrilled to show us how he recently jury-rigged a portable Black & Decker drill to turn the crank when Josephine's arm gets tired.

As we sit in a booth with Lina and listen to her tell how she makes cappelletti, a specialty from her family's homeland in Le Marche, Gary stands by his mother's side, his face lighting up: "*Caplets!*" he exclaims— the familiar term for the pasta called *cappelletti* because they resemble little hats. "She makes the cappelletti so small they are like this!" Gary says, using the thumb and forefinger of his left hand to pinch his right pinkie so only the fingernail shows.

"No!" Mother corrects him, "They are like this." She puts forth her daintier little finger as the measure.

Gary agrees, withdrawing his muscular baker's hands and, exulting about how wonderful it is when she makes her tiny pasta packets, fill- ing hundreds of them with seasoned veal, beef, and pork, and serving them in a bowl of golden chicken broth with a hunk of the good grated cheese on top.

Cappelletti are not often on the menu because they require so much work and such a fine hand, but Lina can sometimes enlist her old kitchen mate Annie, also from Le Marche, to help her; and recently she found another unlikely cappelletti maker. The young apprentice is a boy originally hired to bus tables, a hefty guy with big hands, known to his pals as Flounder, after the chubby frat brother in the movie *Animal House*. Despite his size, Flounder can precisely fold a thin, one-inch pasta square into a triangle, then bring around the corners to form a little hat. Lina laughs out loud at the big boy's knack with the delicate dough. Because she is not all that familiar with American teen movies, she often mistakenly calls him Halibut.

We were rapt as Lina regaled us with family history—her old-coun- try girlhood in a convent where she was placed to protect her from the Fascists; a dramatic midnight escape when Mussolini's men invaded the school; her arrival in America at age seven; childhood winters at the restaurant, which soon expanded to a three-booth establishment, for which ice for cold drinks was retrieved by cutting icicles hanging from the roof outside. Lina's brow darkens as she recalls the two weeks toward the end of World War II when her father closed Roseland because he was so distraught by her older brother's death as a U.S. infantryman in the Battle of the Bulge. "He spent two weeks alone in the garden after that," she says. "I went to him and said, 'Please, come back to the restaurant. I will help you, I will work with you.'" She knew that running the restaurant and working with his family was what her father needed to do to cure the ache of loneliness. "To Italians, family is everything," she explains. "And it is food that holds the family together."

Lina's Cappelletti in Brodo

The art of forming cappelletti is best learned by apprenticing with someone who knows how. It looked so easy as Lina stood next to us and made identical perfect little dough hats in a trice and, with practice, we sort of got the hang of it . . . although every one of our cappelletti had a style all its own! This same good, simple meat filling can also be used to fill much simpler-to-make ravioli. (As this recipe requires so little meat, we suggest using the leftovers from what you buy at the market to make meatloaf or meatballs.)

PASTA DOUGH

1 heaping cup all-purpose flour

$1/2$ teaspoon salt

$1^1/2$ tablespoons olive oil

1 egg

$1/4$ cup water (approximately)

Put the flour in a large mixing bowl. Stir in salt, olive oil, and eggs, then add just enough water to form a stiff dough. Knead until smooth on a floured board. Cover with plastic wrap and allow the dough to rest at least $1/2$ hour. While dough rests, make filling. When ready to make cappelletti, roll the dough out very thin, and cut into $1^1/3$-inch squares.

MEAT FILLING

1 tablespoon butter	$^1/_4$ teaspoon grated nutmeg
$^1/_3$ pound ground meat (equal parts pork, veal, and beef)	Salt and pepper, to taste
Grated rind of 1 lemon	$^1/_3$ cup grated Parmesan

1. Melt butter in a skillet. Sauté meat until browned, breaking it up with a fork until it is fine. When cooked through (about 2 minutes), stir in remaining ingredients, mixing well. Remove from heat and cool. Mash with a fork until it is pasty.

2. To make cappelletti, place a scant teaspoon full of filling in the center of a pasta square. Fold two corners of the square to form a triangle, using a fingertip dipped in water to moisten the dough, so it sticks together. Sweep the other two corners around your pinkie and pinch them together, creating a little hat. Set cappelletti on a lightly floured baking sheet.

3. Cook and serve the cappelletti in a simple chicken stock.

Makes about 4 dozen cappelletti.

Rowe's Restaurant

Mildred Rowe doesn't do everything, all the time, at her restaurant; it only seems that way. Her hospitality, and her expertise as a cook, infuse the Shenandoah Valley way station, which has been in business for more than half a century. Just yards from Interstate 81, Mrs. Rowe's restaurant is a reminder that the word *restaurant* refers to restoring one's self, body and spirit. A visit with Mrs. Rowe is an encounter with a culinary life force that makes the world go round.

She is a small, tidy woman with white hair, a sweet voice burnished by the tender accent of Virginia's western hills, and the piercing gaze of a maestro whose career has been driven by a passion. In her case, the passion is food, served the way she learned when she was a girl growing up in the hills of Alleghany County. As we speak with her at a table in the dining room, a waitress carries past a tray that includes a small bowl of macaroni and cheese, one of about a dozen side dishes on the menu every day. "Ooo, look!" she says, her attention magnetically drawn away from conversation to the mound of golden-orange noodles venting buttery steam, and laced with chewy shreds of cheese from the top of the baked casserole. "Macaroni and cheese!" she exclaims like a thirsty oenophile observing the uncorking of a bottle of 1959 Lafitte Rothschild. "Doesn't that look good?"

Nothing escapes Mrs. Rowe's insistence on doing things right. Buttermilk biscuits are rolled out every morning and brought to the table oven-hot; apple sauce—homemade, of course—is served warm; in the summer, rhubarb cobbler, pie, and bread pudding are made from ripe-that-day stalks she pulls from her home garden. One time a lazy night cook at the restaurant came upon a sample case of instant mashed potatoes that had been left by a salesman. The cook figured he could use the reconstituted potato flakes instead of laboriously making potatoes Mrs.

Rowe's way—peeling, boiling, mashing, mixing. Within minutes of the instant spuds coming into the dining room, Mrs. Rowe knew something was wrong. She marched into the kitchen and heaved the batch of instant potatoes into a dumpster.

Even before the creation of this restaurant, Mildred Rowe was destined for renown. Her first café, opened in the 1940s in the small town of Goshen, was named The Far Famed Restaurant after a customer from California stopped by and declared, "This food is so good that everybody ought to know about it!" Once Mildred married Willard Rowe, proprietor of a forty-five-seat café in Staunton called Perk's Bar-B-Q, the die was cast. She cooked during the day and waitressed at night. Perk's was transformed into Rowe's Steak House. Gradually, more of Mrs. Rowe's strapping specialties were added to the menu, which became an encyclopedia of classic country cooking.

Sustained by locals, who valued the comfort food they found here, and soon discovered by wayfarers along the scenic Blue Ridge Parkway, Rowe's earned a sterling reputation as a home of inexpensive southern meals in a wholesome, comfy setting. For many years it was known as Rowe's Family Restaurant, but recently the word *family* was dropped, because of the suspicious connotations it has assumed in the restaurant business. Mike explains, "Too often, *family* now means a menu of quick-fix meals, sandwiches, and hamburgers, or a sloppy buffet where you have to fight with other customers to get your food. We will never go to buffet-style service here. When mother called this place a family restaurant, she was expressing a degree of civility, as well as the sort of food that families have traditionally gathered around a table to share."

Both Mrs. Rowe and her son Mike agree that one reason the restaurant has been able to consistently maintain its high culinary standards is that employees tend to stay a long time. Many signature dishes not created by Mrs. Rowe herself are the legacy of the late John Morris, Rowe's head cook for thirty-nine years, and of Vivian Obie, now in her forty-seventh year with the family business. Even the dishwashers, Mike notes, all have at least six years on the job—a remarkable statistic for a job that is notoriously transient. Why do employees remain so loyal to Rowe's? Mike explains: "Good benefits, pensions and health plans."

His mother nods her head in agreement, but adds one more logical reason for employee loyalty: "We feed them!"

Mrs. Rowe's Summer Squash Casserole

Many locals come to Rowe's every day at lunch for a vegetable plate: three or four from that day's roster, accompanied by warm dinner rolls and iced tea. In the summer, as gardens ripen, squash casserole is a frequent choice.

2 slices bacon, fried and crumbled (reserve drippings)

6 cups diced summer squash

1 teaspoon beef bouillon granules

$^1/_4$ cup grated onion

1 green pepper, chopped

1 cup sour cream

2 eggs, beaten

$^1/_2$ cup grated sharp cheddar cheese

1 2-ounce jar pimientos, drained

1 cup fresh bread crumbs (or enough to cover casserole)

1. Fry, drain, and crumble bacon, reserving drippings.
2. In a pot or pan, cover the squash with water, add the bouillon, and cook over medium heat until the squash is tender, about twenty minutes.
3. Preheat oven to 350°F.
4. Drain squash and mash it. Add bacon, drippings, and all other ingredients except the bread crumbs. Stir to mix well. Season with salt and pepper. Pour into a buttered casserole dish and top with bread crumbs. Bake one hour, or until bubbly and browned.

Makes 10–12 servings.

Schwabl's

*W*hen you cook a roast the way we do—fast, at a high temperature—it shrinks fifteen or twenty percent," Ray Schwabl says, as he leads us to twin ovens in the tiny kitchen at the back of his fifty-seat restaurant/tavern in Buffalo, New York. "Equipment salesmen are always trying to sell me a modern roaster that would cook the meat with less shrinkage. But I tell them I don't mind that shrinkage. *I need that shrinkage!* And this is why." He opens the oven door, slides out a slow-sizzling roast pan, and lifts its lid. He uses a long spoon to stir the bottom of the pan, which is filling up with amber-hued juice drawn from the roast as it cooks. A concentrated beef aroma swirls up into the air. This protein perfume radiates throughout Schwabl's restaurant all day long. "From these pure beef drippings, I make gravy for the mashed potatoes or to ladle on French fries, and for the roast-beef plates," he says. "And to serve beef on weck right, you *need* the *jus* to moisten the rolls. This is a sandwich that no one orders dry."

Beef on weck is the pride of Buffalo: a heap of slices from an oven-warm round of beef piled into a roll known as a *kümmelweck*, from the German *Kümmel*, meaning caraway seed. The roll resembles a big Kaiser roll, but it is crowned with a mantle of seeds and coarse salt so abundant that it crunches audibly when bitten. It is tawny, with an extraordinarily fine crumb. The roll's gentle texture is crucial, because it is designed to cushion, but not compete, with the gentle feel of the sliced beef. Its top half is customarily immersed in pan juice just long enough for it to start to soften before it is set atop the sandwich. For most Buffalonians, the only possible condiment to consider on this sandwich is horseradish, preferably fresh grated and very hot.

Ray Schwabl is a beef-on-weck expert. His family started in the restaurant trade when his father's great-grandfather, a brewmaster, came to America from Germany in 1837, and sold hot meals with beer from his house. The Schwabls have been restaurateurs ever since. Historians cannot confirm the precise origin of beef on weck, but Ray likes to think that it was at one of their several restaurants in and around Buffalo that hot roast beef first was sandwiched inside kümmelweck rolls, some time in the 'teens or 1920s.

Today, there is only one Schwabl's restaurant, although several other places in town specialize in beef-on-weck sandwiches; Charlie the Butcher and Eckl's are among the best. When you come to Schwabl's, we highly recommend sitting toward the front, or at least waiting at the bar a spell; here, you have a view of the carving board and of Ray or his associates, Dave Brown and Claus Augenreich, making sandwiches. It is enthralling to watch them put their perfectly sharpened knives to the

roast, and to neatly halve the kümmelwecks to be immersed in gravy, a process conducted with such earnestness and dignity that we are reminded of medical professionals at work—an impression abetted by the immaculate white smocks they wear, as well as by the extraordinarily sober tone of the dining room. Although many dinner guests start their meal with expertly made Manhattans, old fashioneds, or whiskey sours, or (in winter) Tom and Jerrys, and cold beer flows as fast as beef is cut, no one comes to Schwabl's only to drink. *We Cater to Nice Homey Family Trade,* the menu announces, and a dry, nonalcoholic birch beer with the faint twang of spearmint is always available on draught for tee-totalers who are given respect along with their weck.

Roast Beef for Beef on Weck

If you aren't a restaurant chef or caterer, you probably don't want to cook a forty-pound round roast, which is what most Buffalo beef-on-weck chefs use. However, a nice eye of round, four to six pounds, works fine for home use. If you want to splurge, nothing makes better beef for sandwiches than a tenderloin. The latter is so lean that it benefits from a layer of fat on top as it roasts. Whatever kind of roast you use, you will need a meat thermometer for perfect control of the meat's done-ness.

1 eye round or tenderloin roast, 4–6 pounds, at room temperature

salt and pepper

1. Preheat oven to 450°F.

2. Place the roast on a shallow rack in a roasting pan (fat-side up, if using a round roast, or tied with suet or bacon, if using a tenderloin). Sprinkle generously with salt and pepper. Add about $^{1}/_{4}$-inch water to the bottom of the pan.

3. Put the roast in the oven, and immediately lower heat to 350°F. Cook until a meat thermometer in the center of the roast reads 120°F, remove the roast from the oven, and let it settle, covered loosely with foil, 10–15 minutes before slicing. (120 is rare, which is traditionally right for beef-on-weck sandwiches. Expect internal temperature to rise about 5 degrees as the roast settles.) Cooking time will vary depending on the thickness of the roast, anywhere from 10–20 minutes per pound.

4. Slice thin for sandwiches, and use the pan gravy to moisten the top half of the kümmelwecks. (You may need to stir a little water into the pan, but do *not* thicken it.)

Makes enough beef for 12 sandwiches.

Quick Kümmelwecks

Charlie Roesch, proprietor of Charlie the Butcher (one of Buffalo's great beef-on-weck restaurants), provided this method for making quick kümmelweck rolls. For those of us who don't have access to a bakery that makes them, it's an essential part of the meal plan.

1 cup water

1 tablespoon cornstarch, dissolved in
 $1/4$ cup water

$1/4$ cup kosher salt, mixed with 2 tablespoons caraway seeds

12 fresh Kaiser rolls

1. Preheat oven to 350°F.

2. Bring water to a boil. Add cornstarch paste to the boiling water. Boil until thickened. Remove from heat. Brush the tops of the Kaiser rolls with this edible glue, and sprinkle with salt-and-caraway-seed mixture. Heat rolls, 3–4 minutes.

Makes 12 rolls.

Snappy Lunch

*C*harles Dowell, who first started working at Snappy Lunch on Main Street of Mount Airy, North Carolina, in 1943, when he was fourteen years old, sees himself heading toward dire straits. Everything is okay for the moment, as long as his Tenderator still works. But, if the Tenderator goes on the blink, he is going to be in big trouble . . . and so will all the loyal customers who depend on Mr. Dowell to use that vintage Tenderator to prepare pork chops the correct way for the Snappy Lunch pork-chop sandwich.

"It can be done with a mallet," says the veteran diner cook, who is never without a white apron tied at his waist and a skiff-shaped, white-paper Sanacap perched atop his head. He reaches deep into an unseen nook in his two-by-four kitchen, and pulls out a giant hammer with a heavy, square head and a ridged face for tenderizing a slab of meat, inspecting the primitive tool with some disdain. "I don't like the way a mallet flattens the pork chop. I also have a fifteen-hundred dollar meat cuber at home that will do the job, but that squeezes the meat too much and makes it dry."

To prove the superiority of his vintage Tenderator, which he discovered many years ago in an antique shop, he takes a trimmed, boneless pork chop, just under an inch thick, and slides it into the top of the small, white-enamel countertop machine. Shaped vaguely like a bread toaster, but with a slot on the bottom as well as the top, the Tenderator grabs the chop and silently pulls it in, moving it top to bottom like a piece of paper going through a shredder. At first glance, the chop that comes out appears unchanged from the chop that went in. However, once it slides into Mr. Dowell's waiting hands, he folds the piece of meat to show that the whirring blades of the Tenderator have cut it with tiny parallel incisions, front and back.

The problem is that Tenderators are no longer made, and parts are not available. So, if you happen to have a Tenderator in your attic, or come across one at a flea market, won't you please call Charles Dowell and figure out a way he can assume possession of it? Snappy Lunch devotees from coast to coast will thank you.

The supertender pork tenderloin is encased in sweet-milk batter, then fried to a crisp, and, because each chop is individually Tenderator-ized and dipped by hand, there are some cross-sections that are mostly meat with just a thin batter shell; other parts are soft batter with just a ribbon of moist pork running through.

Mr. Dowell says that pork-chop sandwiches were popular in local restaurants when he grew up in Mount Airy, but the old-time pork chops were heavily breaded and fried with their bone still in. He recalls, "When you got that sandwich, you spent your time gnawing around the bone. You gnawed and gnawed and you got maybe three good bites. One day after I came to Snappy Lunch, it hit me: I'll just take that bone out. I ordered whole loins and told the butcher to keep the bone. But, still, there was a problem: The boneless chops had tough parts, and the tough parts made them hard to eat. I watched customers tear at a chewy section of their sandwich and sometimes I would see the chop slide right out of its bun! It was so embarrassing. That's when I realized it had to be tenderized."

Experienced pork-chop eaters always order their sandwich at Snappy Lunch *all the way*, which means that five separate condiments are applied: a thick slice of tomato, chopped onion, mustard, cole slaw, and Charles Dowell's special chili sauce.

"Chili is the little thing that turned out big," Mr. Dowell says with a philosophic sense of amazement. "It was chili that made the pork-chop sandwich skyrocket. And, the strange thing is that I learned to make it by accident. Once I started serving pork chops, in nineteen and sixty-one, I had a tomato-based chili sauce that I put on them, but there were customers that teased me about it. 'This is not chili!' they'd say. 'It's chili juice.' And they were right. It was so thin, it ran right off the pork chops. I was ashamed. I stood at the grill one day and said to myself, *I've got to thicken it up.* So, I took a little of everything that was on the grill—pork chops, ham, sausage, hamburger, tenderloin; eight different kinds of meat altogether—and ran them all through the food processor with toma-toes. It was thick, and it was good, and it made all the difference. Now everybody wants to buy my chili by the quart, but I can barely make enough for the pork chops we serve in the restaurant."

The chili, which has the consistency of chili paste, and a sweet zest that serves as a foil for the creamy chop, makes Mr. Dowell's amazing sandwich unwieldy in the extreme. Served in booths or at the counter with no plate, but with a wax paper wrapper that serves as a holding place for fallen condiments, a Snappy Lunch pork-chop sandwich requires two hands to hoist and eat. Dainty eaters use the plastic knife and fork pro-vided to cut the sandwich in half, but even half is inevitably messy. There are no side dishes other than a bag of potato chips, and the beverage of choice is tea—iced, of course, the small-town Southern way.

Long before Charles Dowell perfected the pork-chop sandwich, Snappy Lunch was a narrow working man's lunch counter with no seats at all. The all-male clientele stood to eat their food and, when they were finished eating, they threw napkins and sandwich wrappers on the floor. Adjacent to the restaurant was a shoe store. "When the shoemaker cranked up his machines, coffee mugs shimmied off the counter," Mr. Dowell recalls of the days he started as a diswasher. The original menu was little more than bologna sandwiches and breaded hamburgers, a Depression-era dish for which ground beef was extended by mixing it with an equal portion of moistened bread. (To meet old-time customer demand, the breaded burger is still on the menu—a strange spherical patty that looks like a crabcake and is definitely an acquired taste, although the addition of chili and slaw makes it quite accessible.) After starting as a dishwasher and general cleanup man in his teens, then acquiring a half interest in the business in 1951, Mr. Dowell yearned to add niceties to the menu, such as lettuce and tomato garnishes for sandwiches, but his part-ner was a hard case who would not suffer any such frippery.

In 1961, he bought the business, and notes that soon after he added lettuce and tomato to the kitchen's larder, more women started coming in to eat. In the mid-1960s when the shoe store moved out, Snappy Lunch expanded, annexing another narrow dining area where a handful of little booths with school-desk-sized tables were lined up behind the counter.

The cozy storefront still radiates an old-time blue-collar charm, where it is impossible to feel secluded. When you dine at Snappy Lunch, you sit shoulder to shoulder with citizens of Mount Airy, as well as tourists who have come to town because Mount Airy is where television's Andy Griffith actually grew up; it is the real-life inspiration for Andy's fictional home town, Mayberry. (Next door to Snappy Lunch, at Floyd's Barber Shop, seasoned haircutter Russell Hiatt boasts that he used to cut young Andy's hair. Today, for six dollars, he or his niece Donna George will give you a magnificent flattop or regular man's haircut. It's two dollars extra for fragrant hair tonic or a shampoo, four dollars for a shave.)

"We have the most diversified people come to eat with us," Charles Dowell marvels. "Doctors, lawyers, tourists, beggars, ladies and gentlemen, and others, too." His explanation for the little restaurant's huge popularity is the pork-chop sandwich: "You could go all over town looking for a pork chop like this and never find one," he says. We agree. The sandwich is unique, and it is magnificent. However, it takes more than a glorified pork chop to generate the kind of allure radiated by this little diner on Main Street. Snappy Lunch serves each of its customers a generous helping of small-town America, and that is a tasty dish that's getting mighty hard to find.

Snappy Lunch Pork-Chop Sandwich

Even without a Tenderator and a supply of Charles Dowell's chili and slaw, you can make a fine pork chop following his recipe. The ideal piece of meat is a 3/4-inch thick boneless pork chop, four to six inches in diameter after it is tenderized. You can tenderize it by pounding with a mallet, but don't flatten it too much. Charles Dowell suggests that the same batter, just a wee bit thinner, is great for fried onion rings.

2 cups all-purpose flour

2 tablespoons sugar

1/4 teaspoon salt

2 eggs, beaten

1 cup (approximately) milk

Oil, for frying

6 boneless pork chops, trimmed of fat and tenderized

6 hamburger buns

Condiments of choice

1. Mix flour, sugar, and salt. Stir in eggs. Add milk gradually, and beat to create a smooth batter. The batter should run slowly off a spoon, but be thick enough to cling to a pork chop.

2. Heat about $^1/_4$-inch oil in a heavy skillet to medium hot. Too-hot oil will scorch the breading before the meat is cooked.

3. Pat each pork chop to dry thoroughly. Dip it fully into the batter and lay it in the hot oil. Cook, 8–10 minutes per side, turning a few times, until the crust is golden brown.

4. Drain on paper towels and serve on burger buns, dressed with your choice of tomato, onion, mustard, cole slaw, fine-grind all-meat chili, or relish.

Makes 6 sandwiches.

Sophie's Busy Bee

CHICAGO, ILLINOIS

Chicago has more citizens of Polish descent than any other city but Warsaw, Poland. On the northwest side, along Milwaukee Avenue—nicknamed Polish Broadway—corner groceries sell *pierogi* (stuffed dumplings) and *pochke* (plum-filled donuts), and snug little family-run restaurants perfume the street with the smells of sweet czarina soup and sizzling potato pancakes.

In a neighborhood called Wicker Park, one block from where Milwaukee crosses North Avenue, there is a storefront café called Sophie's Busy Bee. Although its pierogi are divine, the Busy Bee is far more than just another place to eat excellent Polish food.

It is an experience that is heart-and-soul Chicago: deeply ethnic, but with a melting-pot hospitality that attracts all cultural groups, and customers from high and low. Any morning, at the big horseshoe counter in the old dining room, you might see longhairs studying the morning papers, blue-collar workmen with heavy tool belts on their waists, amateur philosophers holding forth about issues of the day, artists who work in nearby loft space, families of newcomers from the old country, yuppies buying handsome stone houses to renovate, and old-timers who have never left.

"This is America!" proclaims Vic Giustino, a freelance historian specializing in Chicago's character and characters. Vic is a Sophie's regular, whom we meet one morning as the nine-to-five crowd at the counter gives way to those customers getting off the night shift or with their morning free. He gazes with hometown pride across the clamorous dining room, in which we can discern conversations carried on in English, Polish, Yiddish, Spanish, and Italian. "What a magnificent conglomeration!" he muses, then commences reeling off some of the significant things that have happened in the Wicker Park neighborhood:

"Paderewski played the piano on the balcony around the corner . . . the St. Valentine's Day Massacre car was found nearby . . . Nelson Algren lived just down the street, and got chased back and forth by Simone de Beauvoir. This is Main Street, U.S.A., and the Busy Bee is its crossroads."

Mr. Giustino also reminds us about the dramatic fall and rise of Wicker Park. When Sophie Madej bought the Busy Bee in 1965, the neighborhood was a safe and happy place. Riots in the wake of Martin

Luther King Jr.'s assassination in 1968 destroyed it, causing many of the old residents and business owners to flee. Vic then turns over the story of the neighborhood's tumultuous fate to his breakfast partner, a fellow history buff named William Jaconetti. Jaconetti is a uniformed police officer whose beat includes the Busy Bee. "I have been with Sophie thirty-one years," he boasts of his longstanding status as a regular customer. "I have seen Wicker Park go from one of the most depraved, violent areas in the country to one of the best, a place where everybody now wants to buy a house. And Sophie has stayed through it all. I honestly believe that if she hadn't stuck to her guns, there would be no Wicker Park as we know it today. Without the presence of Sophie's Busy Bee, this neighborhood would have died."

Back in the early 1970s, when things were bad, Sophie's friends and relatives told her to get out while she could. "Where am I going to go?" she answered them. For Sophie, who had come to America in 1951 as a postwar refugee, then spent ten years working in the bone-numbing cold of a meat-packing plant, owning the Busy Bee was a dream come true, a dream she had no intention of giving up. It was back in those troubled days she got to know Officer Jaconetti, then on his first assignment—to clean up the neighborhood.

"There was nowhere else to eat," Jaconetti recalls. "Sophie was the only person who had the courage to keep her business open and, because she did, all the police came in here, and this got to be a kind of hangout for us. But even that didn't stop the bad guys. I have chased them right through this restaurant, and I've had shootouts in the street."

At this point, Vic Giustino pulls one of us aside, so as not to embarrass his friend when he points out that William Jaconetti is a holder of the Lambert Tree medal, Chicago's highest award for bravery, and one of his bullet-riddled jackets is on display in the police museum. Jaconetti's combat experience has taught him to pack a pair of revolvers, one on each hip, just in case one hand is incapacitated in a fight.

Now that Wicker Park has been revitalized and the real estate is prime, Sophie's Busy Bee is still a favorite haunt of the Chicago police; it is rare to come in any time of day and not see at least one uniformed officer at the counter or in a booth. "This just might be the safest place in Chicago," Officer Jaconetti says with a knowing smile.

It is also one of the most colorful places in Chicago, the sort of restaurant politicians like to visit during a campaign to show they are in touch with real people. "Hillary Clinton was standing right here when she said she would not stay home and bake cookies," Vic Giustino notes, recalling the First Lady's controversial statement of principle in 1992.

We reckon that a lot of people come to Sophie's to sate a hunger for something other than food. When she is present in the dining room, there is hardly a single customer who comes or goes, whether old friend or newcomer, that she doesn't greet with genuine warmth and interest. As in any big family, there are some she cherishes—such as the police officers who make camp at the counter—and there are others who never seem to leave—like the two eccentric old Wicker Park ladies who occupy a booth at 9 AM, and spend three hours toying with their pancakes—but they are her people, one and all, and it is this gathering of characters that makes Sophie's Busy Bee such a special place.

As we leave the café one morning, we notice Officer Jaconetti at the counter talking in whispers to a man in a suit, clearly a plainclothes detective. The gumshoe follows us out the door. On the sidewalk, he sidles close and, without introduction or explanation, gives us the scoop under his breath: "Any cop who eats Dunkin' Donuts when he could be at Sophie's needs to have his head examined."

Sophie's closed in 1999, as Wicker Park grew ever more fashionable, and real estate in the once-foundering neighborhood skyrocketed in value.

Sophie's Polish Chop Suey

The Busy Bee menu was different every day, so that regulars could enjoy a variety of lunches throughout the week. One of the favorite dishes in rotation was Sophie's Polish Chop Suey. It sure isn't Polish, nor is it Chinese, and it doesn't even bear much resemblance to any Chinese-American chop suey we've ever encountered. Talk about a melting-pot meal!

1 cup chopped onion

3 cloves garlic, minced

5 tablespoons vegetable oil

1/3 cup all-purpose flour

1 teaspoon pepper

1 tablespoon salt

1 pound lean pork loin, cut into ?-inch cubes

1 pound veal stew meat, trimmed of fat and cut into 1/2-inch cubes

2 cups water

3 tablespoons soy sauce

2 tablespoons molasses

2 ribs celery, diced

1 cup fresh bean sprouts

1/2 cup chopped parsley

Rice or chow-mein noodles, for serving

1. Preheat oven to 350°F.

2. In a Dutch oven or heavy pot, sauté the onion and garlic in the cooking oil until soft.

3. Add pepper and salt to the flour. Dredge meat in seasoned flour. Add meat to the sautéed onions and braise over medium-high heat until it is well-browned on all sides, turning frequently.

4. Add water, soy sauce, and molasses, cover the pot, and place in the preheated oven, 30 minutes, stirring occasionally. Remove the lid, stir in the celery, bean sprouts, and parsley. Continue cooking in the oven, uncovered, 45 minutes more, stirring occasionally.

5. Serve over white rice or chow-mein noodles.

Makes 6 servings.

Stone's Restaurant

MARSHALLTOWN, IOWA

*A*slice of Stone's lemon-chiffon pie seems to defy the laws of physics. You wonder, when you see it being carried to the table by a waitress, how on earth they do it, and how it stays in one piece, considering the fact that each slice is about ten inches tall.

It is an incredible piece of pie, but the best thing about it is that if you cannot get to the heart of Iowa to eat it at Stone's, it is easy to make at home. If you are a reasonably accomplished hand about the kitchen, you, too, can amaze your family and friends with mile-high pie, just like the ones they have been serving here in Marshalltown since the 1930s.

Actually, the restaurant goes back way before that. Stone's was started in 1887, serving passers-by on the nearby railroad, but it was in 1937, that Anna N. Stone, widow of the son of the founder, added the famous lemon pie to the menu and changed what was a journeyman's restaurant into a daintier one suitable for the fair sex as well as passing gentlemen. It stayed in the Stone family until 1979, when long-time employee Elaine Fearnow took the reins. When you dine at Stone's today, there is a real sense of continuity about the meal.

First, you have to find Stone's. If you are a stranger in Marshalltown, that isn't easy. It is way down under the viaduct for the new highway, not in any kind of normal business district. Nonetheless, when we finally came upon it around noontime, there was hardly a place to park, and the vintage three-room restaurant was packed with locals.

Fans spin overhead in the first long room, where a U-shaped counter seats singles and a few couples who enjoy side-by-side dining. Back in the other two rooms, the atmosphere is more genteel. We were seated by an alcove with a trellis, flowers, a birdcage with a couple of stuffed budgies inside, and a light that glowed pink for atmosphere.

The menu is all-American fare, including sandwiches, salads, and hot plate lunches, such as liver and onions, grilled steak, meatloaf with

mashed potatoes, and pork roast. All the hot meals are accompanied by creamy, fresh cole slaw, hot dinner rolls, and some delicious-smelling cornbread.

There are other things to eat for dessert, including grasshopper pie, cheese-cake, and a mighty tasty turtle pie (that's chocolate, caramel, and ice cream), but you've got to get that mile-high pie, if only just to gape at it. And if you aren't going to be visiting central Iowa soon, here's the authentic recipe, courtesy of Stone's.

Mile High Lemon-Chiffon Pie

8 egg yolks, slightly beaten

1 cup sugar

Juice of 2 lemons

2 lemon rinds, grated

Pinch salt

2 tablespoons unflavored gelatin

½ cup cold water

8 egg whites, at room temperature

1 cup sugar

1 fully baked 9-inch pie crust

Whipped cream, for serving

1. In the top of a double boiler, over simmering water, cook egg yolks, sugar, lemon juice, rind, and salt. Stir constantly, cooking until mixture is the consistency of a thick custard.

2. Soak gelatin in cold water until dissolved. Stir into hot custard. Let cool.

3. Place egg whites in a mixing bowl and set the bowl in another bowl of very warm (but not boiling) water. Beat egg whites until stiff but not dry. Gradually beat in sugar. Fold completely cooled custard into beaten egg whites. Pile into prepared pie crust and smooth into a dome shape. Chill 3 full hours. Serve dolloped with whipped cream.

Makes 1 nine-inch pie.

The Sycamore Drive-In

BETHEL, CONNECTICUT

Pull into the parking lot of the Sycamore Drive-In and flash your lights. In a jiffy, a carhop will be at your car window. Place your order and, a few minutes after that, out comes the carhop once again, this time toting a tray full of food to attach to the window. Turn up the radio and dine in style in the comfort of your front seat.

Welcome to one of the last genuine drive-in restaurants. Name your burger, and they make it here: with or without cheese, smothered with onions, stacked up double-decker style, plain or fancy. These are some swell hamburgers. They are not gourmet thick or yuppie elegant. They are cooked in a manner the menu describes as "French-style," but, to us, it looks classically American. That is, they are squished flat with a heavy spatula.

If you ever go inside the Sycamore (there are booths and counter seats, too), you can watch the man at the grill make the burgers, and it is a real education in hamburgerology. When one is ordered, the chef grabs a big round gob of ground beef and slams it down on the hot grill. He then immediately presses it down hard, flattening it into a vaguely round patty, so thin at the outer edges that you can practically see through it. The center remains somewhat thicker, perhaps a quarter inch, but not much more than that. The first side of this flattened patty cooks until it is crusty brown, thus the other side barely needs any time on the grill at all, because it has virtually cooked through. The result is a skinny hamburger with one soft, tender side and one wickedly crisp one: a tantalizing configuration, especially if you get two such patties on one bun, the layers of meat festooned with melted American cheese. The doubling up provides a memorable textural variety as you sink your teeth into the hefty sandwich.

To go with your hamburger, you want French fries (which are better than the fairly ordinary onion rings) and a root beer. They actually make their own root beer at the Sycamore, and they serve it in big, chilled mugs that arrive at your car (or table or counter seat) encased in a lovely sheen of frost. Depending on whether your serving comes from the top or bottom

of the barrel, it can range from sugar sweet to elegantly dry. Whatever the vintage, it is good root beer, and a perfect companion for a hamburger.

There are other things on the Sycamore menu, including hot dogs (good ones), chili, and breakfast, even salads. To be honest, we have never had a salad at the Sycamore, and we don't intend to. How could one possibly fork into a bowl of lettuce with a steering wheel in the way?

Dagwoodburgers

1 pound lean ground steak	Mayonnaise
Butter and oil, for frying	9 pickle slices
6 slices American cheese	3 thin slices onion
3 hamburger buns	3 slices tomato
Mustard	$^1/_3$ cup shredded lettuce
Catsup	

1. Separate the meat into six spheres. Each should be a little bigger than a golf ball.

2. In a large skillet or on a griddle, heat equal amounts of butter and oil over medium-high heat. When butter is melted, and sizzling vigorously, place the patties in the oil one by one, flattening each down hard with a spatula until it is no more than $1/4$-inch thick in the center. Cook until the top begins to turn from pink to grey, then flip (taking care not to break the crisp edges of the patties), and drape each with a slice of cheese. Lower heat.

3. Slather each bun with mustard, catsup, and mayonnaise, then arrange pickle, onion, tomato, and lettuce.

4. When cheese on burgers begins to melt, place two patties on each prepared bun. Serve immediately.

Makes 3 Dagwoodburgers.

Threadgill's

AUSTIN, TEXAS

When we cater an event, there seems to be a magnetic force field around our food," observed Eddie Wilson, a swamp-voiced, Mississippi-born Texan, who runs Threadgill's restaurant in Austin. We spoke with Wilson at a party, as he watched hankering Texans crowd around buffet tables set with seafood jambalaya, San Antonio squash, spinach casserole, yeast rolls, and Texas caviar (black-eyed peas marinated with red onions and peppers). "Wherever we go, if we are catering an event with any kind of free access, we always bring two to three times more food than is required for the number of people expected," Eddie explained. "I don't know how it happens, but there are always more mouths to feed than anybody anticipates. And I don't like to see people hungry."

One thing is certain: No one who eats at Threadgill's restaurant up at the north end of Austin could possibly complain about being hungry. Portions are gargantuan. Cornbread squares overlap the plate on which they are presented. Meatloaf is massively sliced, and smothered with chunky Creole sauce. Sheaves of smoked and glazed ham are piled on a plate under a great spill of Jezebel sauce (named for its seductive sweet-and-tart blend of horseradish, mustard, and apple jelly). And the deep-fried chicken-liver platter is one of the most astounding plates of food available anywhere, described on the menu as "more than anyone can eat!" It is a mountain of golden-crusted livers bigger than half a basket-ball, perhaps two or three dozen of them, so gnarled and knobby you can almost see them puffing up and exploding when they hit the hot fat just a few minutes before. The plate itself is oversized, so it also has room for mashed potatoes, maybe a couple of cups' worth, blanketed with thick, peppery cream gravy. On the side: more gravy in a wide bowl, for dipping. Eddie Wilson gleefully tells how a friend of his, a customer and also a cardiologist, gaped at the fried chicken-liver platter coming from the kitchen one day, and declared that its cholesterol count exceeded the maximum recommended monthly dose for any human being.

Incredibly, portions of most things at Threadgill's are *smaller* than they used to be. Eddie explains: "My accountants sat me down, and said this place was going to go down the tubes unless I raised my prices or cut the amount of food we served. I hated to do either, so I thought about it long and hard. The solution came when I heard my mama's voice calling

to me out of the past. She was saying, 'Second helpings?' And I knew what to do. I had to beat the kitchen staff with blunt instruments to get them to change their ways and dish out smaller portions of all our side dishes, but they learned to do it. And now, when the waitress carries food to the table, she tells everyone that second helpings are free. Only five to six percent of our customers have enough appetite for seconds, but they are happy to be asked, and they are so pleased with the waitress for asking that tips have gone way up. Everybody's happy, even my accountants."

Not all the Texas-sized helpings of food Threadgill's serves are as nutritionally wicked as the chicken-liver platter. The specialty of the house is vegetables; although many of them are cooked southern style, meaning profusely enriched with cheese and butter and bread crumbs, several dishes might please even a fastidious dieter. All summer, when the weather has been right for growing, sliced tomatoes from Eddie and his wife Sandra's garden are available: big, plump, flavorful beefsteaks of a quality that is hard enough to find in any pricey epicurean grocery store, let alone a roadside restaurant where the check for an average meal is well under ten dollars. Crunchy okra is stewed in a snapping fresh tomato sauce. Black-eyed peas are simple beauties, scented merely with onion and garlic. Vegetarian jambalaya is a luscious mix of yellow rice, bits of hot jalapeño pepper, cauliflower, tomatoes, squash, and bell pepper. Creole cabbage is simmered in a zesty sauce made from tomatoes smoked in Threadgill's kitchen.

Our own personal preference on the vegetable roster is garlic cheese grits. Custardy, with only a muted garlic punch, they are supreme southern-style nursery food. San Antonio squash, available only on Sunday, Monday, and Tuesday, is another comfortable classic. It is a sumptuous baked casserole of mild cheese, hot chili peppers, onions, and bread crumbs. Also on the seriously luscious list is spinach casserole (Tuesday, Wednesday, Saturday), in which the limp green leaves are sodden with melted Swiss cheese and flavored with chunks of mushroom, bits of onion, and bacon.

Victory with Vegetables says the side of the menu where the twenty-three different side dishes Threadgill's offers every day are listed. Many customers come only to eat side dishes, and lots of them: a selection of three, five, or nine, all of them except the likker-soaked greens (which get their own bowl), heaped together on a single oval trencher like great colorful gobs of paint on an exuberant artist's palette. "Someone calculated that there were 15,553 different combinations available," Eddie Wilson gloats. "I've never checked it out, but there is definitely more choice than in a Chinese restaurant." One lunch hour, we sat near a healthy-looking woman who was eating alone in a booth. She had no book or newspaper, nothing to distract her from her meal, which was a Threadgill's specialty, listed on blackboards in the dining room that day as a "nine-vegetable orgy." She plowed through it all, then had second helpings of ham-flavored butter beans, chili beans, broccoli-and-rice casserole, and bacony turnip greens, all the while going through about eight refill glasses of iced tea and two platters of bread.

Good as the vegetables may be, it would be a big mistake to come to Threadgill's and not eat meat, too, preferably something chicken fried, meaning dipped and breaded and quickly cooked in a vat of hot oil. The menu lists a chicken-fried pork chop and chicken-fried chicken breast, but the item you want to zero in on is the southwestern paradigm:

chicken-fried steak. There is none better. That's because, according to Eddie Wilson, "Everybody else does it wrong. The usual method is dry-wet-dry—dip the meat in flour, then egg wash, then flour again, then throw it in the hot oil. The problem with that technique is that flour on the outside of the steak absorbs so much grease. What do you have? A greasy chicken-fried steak, the kind no one likes. We, on the other hand, go wet-dry-wet—egg wash, flour, then egg wash again. It is wet when it hits the grease. It splatters something awful and makes a terrible noise and a mess, but you get such a nice crusty seal with all the flavor locked inside. And the steak isn't greasy."

Chicken-Fried Steak

6 cube steaks

2 beaten eggs

1 12-ounce can evaporated milk

1 cup all-purpose flour, mixed with
2 teaspoons pepper and
1 teaspoon salt

Lard or vegetable oil, for frying

1 cup milk, mixed with $^1/_4$ cup beef
stock

Salt and pepper, to taste

Mashed potatoes and biscuits, for
serving

1. Sandwich each steak between pieces of wax paper, and beat with a blunt instrument until steaks are about $^1/_4$-inch thick, about 2–3 minutes.

2. Combine the eggs and evaporated milk, and thoroughly soak the steaks in this mixture.

3. Dredge each steak in the seasoned flour, coating it thoroughly. Return to evaporated milk, then dust with remaining seasoned flour.

4. Put enough lard or oil in a deep skillet so there is over $^1/_2$-inch. Heat until it is 360°F.

5. Stand back and ease each steak into the hot oil (it will splatter!). Do not crowd steaks in the skillet. Cook each steak about 4 minutes, or until golden brown on the bottom. Turn, and cook the other side, about 3 more minutes, or until well-browned. Remove steaks from oil with tongs or a slotted spoon and drain on paper towels.

6. Pour off all but 2–3 tablespoons of the oil in the skillet. Return the skillet to the heat, and sprinkle 2 tablespoons seasoned flour over the hot oil, stirring constantly for a full minute, scraping the bottom of the skillet as you stir.

7. Gradually add milk and beef stock, stirring constantly. Continue cooking and stirring, until the gravy is thick. Add salt and pepper, to taste.

8. Serve with mashed potatoes and biscuits.

Makes 6 steaks.

Garlic Cheese Grits

3 cups cooked grits, still warm

2 eggs, beaten

$^1/_4$ cup milk

$^3/_4$ cup Jack cheese, shredded

$^1/_4$ cup finely minced sweet onion

2 tablespoons melted butter

1–2 cloves minced garlic, to taste

1 teaspoon salt

1. Preheat oven to 350°F.

2. Combine all ingredients, and pour into a well-buttered 6-cup casserole. Bake 1 hour.

Makes 6 servings.

Tigua Reservation Cafeteria

EL PASO, TEXAS

The Tigua Indian Reservation is in downtown El Paso, just across the border from Juarez, and light years away from sophisticated Dallas or Houston. This is a city with a distinctly foreign flavor, and a mystery about it that can appear impenetrable to the casual visitor. Here, it seems, life happens behind closed doors, for the streets look deserted much of the day, and the stores look shuttered even when they are open for business. Tigua Indians live all around the town, but their cultural center is in a somewhat ramshackle neighborhood behind a big adobe wall that, like so much else in the city, gives the impression of a mystery tucked away from view.

The Tiguas (pronounced *tee-wah*) are best known to the outside world for their pottery, which is thin-walled and intricately coiled. Once it is fired, it is hand painted with geometric designs in black and white. Occasionally, you will see some dark red in the decoration—a stripe, an image of a parrot, or a dog. The red used to remind us of the color of the Texas earth at sunset. Now it makes us think only of one thing: chili.

It was on our first visit to El Paso, back in 1976, that we encountered Tigua chili, which set the standard by which we have judged chili ever since. It also taught us a lesson in culinary humility.

We were on the road west hunting restaurants for the first edition of *Roadfood*. Someone had tipped us off about the Tigua reservation and, Jane, a fanatic about all things Indian, insisted that we stop to have a look. Michael was appeased to find that the showroom of Tigua crafts was adjacent to a small cafeteria that server food to tribespeople. We were the only non-Indians lining up with trays in our hands at 11:30 AM when the dining room opened.

It was a simple, working-person's lunch room. Unlike the mighty Navajos or the casino-millionaire Mashentucket Peqouts, the Tiguas are not rich and powerful. They are a small, inner-city tribe that hang together through the cultural ritual of breaking bread together, in this case, Indian fry bread. The menu at the cafeteria consisted of three things, four if you included desert: mild green chili, hot red chili, a piece of fry bread, and a rough-hewn Indian version of rice pudding, called *capirotada*. Jane, whose spirit was already soaring from buying three fabulous Tigua pots, had worked up a big appetite. She grabbed a tray and was ready to eat.

"Which chili is the hot one?" she asked the small plump lady with the ladle behind the serving pots. The little lady pointed to the vat of cinnabar red stew. "Good!" Jane motioned. "That is the one I want. A large bowl, please."

We did not realize we were being observed when we ordered, but silently a large man appeared next to us and shook his head at the serving lady to indicate *no*. We had no idea who he was. He was obviously an Indian, a Tigua, we assumed. His long black hair was tied in a ponytail and, on both hands, he wore big silver bracelets with old green-blue stones. He shook his head again and addressed the lady with the ladle: "Mamie, give her the other chili, the green one."

Jane looked aghast at this man's intrusion.

He spoke before she could. "That red chili is very hot. You won't like it."

Jane looked him up and down. Her eyes narrowed and her shoulders stiffened. As a long-time connoisseur of hot foods, she prided herself on an ability to cook and eat the hottest. She had grown up in southern Arizona, and had seen a few chilies in her day. Obviously, this poor, confused soul had mistaken her for a tourist.

"You see, this chili is cooked to the Tigua taste," the man continued. He explained that he was the chili cook himself. It was his job to arrive in the kitchen at 6 AM, scorch and peel the fresh chilies, puree them with a handful of other secret ingredients, then brew the fiery stuff until lunch, when it was fit to be served to his people. His position as chili maker was a lofty one, and he was also the tribal chief. He handed us a business card with his name on it: Jose Sierra.

Jane was impressed that he was the tribal chief, but she was not about to back down from her lunch order. She could see others getting bowls full of the grainy red stew, sided with a cushiony piece of fry bread that came straight from the wood-fired *horno* oven out back. "I am quite sure I would like a bowl of the red chili," she insisted, refusing to move along the cafeteria line. Finally, Jose Sierra gave the ladle-lady a nod and Jane was given her order. We walked back to a table in the little dining room—a picnic-style table where we sat with four strangers, all Tiguas who spooned up their red chili with gusto.

"Do you mind if I join you?" Jose Sierra asked, sitting down at the end of the table, as he watched Jane with a broad grin on his face. He was waiting for her to dip in, and she knew it. To annoy him, she slowly chewed the fry bread, sipped at her Coke, and delayed the moment. Finally she took a spoonful—a big, hearty spoonful. Not just Jose Sierra, but all eyes at that table were on her. She did her best to chew the tiny cubes of beef that dotted the thick grainy red chili, but as she chewed her face began to redden, her nose began to run, and her eyes teared. It was hot. It was hotter than any food she had ever eaten. Hotter than any food that she had ever cooked. On a scale of one to ten, this was in the triple digits. It was like eating fire. Finally, grabbing a wad of napkins from the dispenser on the table, Jane held them to her mouth and swallowed the best she could, and then started to cough and sputter. Suddenly the kind hands of good Samaritans were pushing fry bread at her, a glass of milk, more Coke, and some rice pudding. All the while Jose Sierra sat there with something more subtle than an I-told-you-so look, clearly enjoying the hell out of this. Jane had just endured the Tigua Indian version of the old cowboy trick of putting the know-it-all city slicker on the wildest bronco at the ranch, then letting the fun begin.

When Jane could breathe again, and had regained the power of speech, she admitted that she had not ever encountered anything this fiery, then decided to have another go at it. Tiny spoonful by tiny spoonful, she let the chili sit in her mouth, and soon, beneath the fire, she got the taste that made Jose Sierra's chili so popular with his tribe. Like all great chili chefs, this man was an artist, and had created a dish that, despite its ferocity, teased the tongue with an earthy, sunny flavor. He explained that his grandfather taught him how to grow and harvest the red and green pods, and how to char the skins just so, and how to cook the chilies with meat until they are perfect. We asked him for the recipe, which he wrote down on a napkin for us before we left. We still have that napkin, with the little red smudges on it from being held in Jane's chili-stained fingers, and we now know better than to challenge a Tigua Indian at high noon under the scorching El Paso sun.

Tigua Indian Chili

4 whole dried chipotle chilies

8 whole fresh Anaheim or New Mexico chilies

4 tablespoons lard

6 garlic cloves, minced

1 cup minced onion

4 pounds lean chuck steak, cut into $1/2$-inch cubes

2 tablespoons ground cumin

1 tablespoon ground jalapeño pepper[*]

1 teaspoon oregano

2–3 teaspoons salt, to taste

2 teaspoons coarse-ground black pepper

2 bay leaves

2 cups water, or less

1 tablespoon masa harina, mixed with $1/4$ cup water, to form a paste

1. Immerse the chipotle chilies in boiling water for 30 minutes or until softened.

2. As the chipotles soften, prepare the Anaheim chilies. In a broiler or over an open flame, char the chilies, so that the skin is singed but the flesh does not burn. When they are blackened all over, wrap each in a moistened paper towel. When cool enough to handle, peel off the burnt skin, tear the pod open, and scoop out and discard all seeds, as well as the stems.

3. Remove the stems and seeds from the softened chipotles. (Be sure to use rubber gloves when handling these peppers; they are very hot!)

4. In a food processor, combine the chili flesh with $1/2$ cup water. Puree.

5. Melt the lard in a deep, heavy skillet or Dutch oven. Sauté garlic and onion until soft, but not browned. Add beef and sauté, until thoroughly browned all over, about 10 minutes.

6. Add the chili puree, and remaining spices, along with 1 cup water. Bring to boil, lower heat, cover and simmer, stirring occasionally, 2 full hours. Add water as necessary to keep the chili moist.

7. When meat is very, very tender, stir in the masa harina paste to thicken the chili.

8. Remove bay leaves and serve with discs of fry bread for mopping the bowl.

Makes 8 servings.

*Ground jalapeño pepper is available from Chile Today Hot Tamale: 1-800-HOT-PEPPER or at www.chiletoday.com

Ulbrick's

*I*t was a sad day in August 2000, when Ulbrick's closed its doors for good. For many years, this was the place people in the midlands went for a rollicking good time and four-star chicken dinners.

Ulbrick's did not look like a four-star eatery, not by a jugful. It was, in fact, a former gas station that, to be frank, always looked like a dump. Even when you walked in the door, you didn't see anything in the way of linen napery or lovely table settings, fine art on the walls, or gleaming crystal. What you did see was a counter in what used to be the front of the gas station, and a rather cozy room in back: the main dining room. The place was decorated in a style described by our very polite Midwestern lady friend as "clutter decor." Did that ever dissuade Mrs. Propriety from eating at Ulbrick's? Not on your life. She, like so many folks along the Iowa–Nebraska border, loved the old place just the way it was, mismatched chairs and all.

The cause for customers' affection was simple, and can be expressed in three words: *fried-chicken dinners*. We thought about shortening it to two words—*fried chicken*—which is moist and succulent inside its well-seasoned, golden-crisp crust, cooked in pure lard in a big old skillet, but that would have left out a lot of the reason people loved coming to Ulbrick's and putting on the feedbag: the vegetables served along with the chicken.

First, potatoes. For decades, Ulbrick's was known for mashed potatoes, and the first person who told us about this out-of-the-way eatery sang praises of those spuds. Alas, he said, they stopped serving mashed potatoes at some time, except on Sunday, and went to French fries. What a tragedy, we thought but, one evening when we asked our waitress about this loss, she said in no uncertain terms—and we quote precisely: "Potatoes are immaterial to us. What we care about are vegetables."

Oh, such vegetables, the likes of which our moms never made! Rich and creamy, every bit as luscious as mashed potatoes, and glorious companions for the brittle-skinned chicken. The every-evening repertoire included creamed corn, creamed cabbage, thick homemade noodles,

green beans, French fries, and dinner rolls. To be honest, we hardly touched our French fries but, to be even more honest, we would have liked to return to Ulbrick's on a Sunday, for the full-bore meal including a mountain of mashed potatoes alongside the creamed cabbage, noodles, corn, and chicken. Sunday dinner couldn't get much better!

The following is a pretty simple recipe for creamed cabbage, which is a fine companion for chicken cooked any which way. It can easily be transformed into the foundation of a one-dish meal by adding such ingredients as chunks of cooked ham and potatoes, spicy discs of grilled kielbasa, or leftover shreds of just about any well-spiced meat.

Creamed Cabbage

3 tablespoons butter

3 tablespoons all-purpose flour

1½ cups hot milk

1½ teaspoons prepared mustard

Pinch cayenne pepper

Salt and pepper, to taste

1 2-pound head white cabbage, trimmed of outer leaves

1 cup dry bread crumbs

2 tablespoons butter

1. In a heavy-bottomed saucepan, melt butter over medium heat. Sprinkle in flour, stirring constantly, as the sauce bubbles and cooks, about 2 minutes. Do not let it brown. Stir in hot milk, continuing to stir as sauce thickens. Bring to a boil. Add mustard, cayenne, and salt and pepper to taste. Lower heat and cook, stirring constantly, 3 more minutes. Remove from heat.

2. Preheat oven to 400°F.

3. Cut cabbage into 8 wedges. Cook in boiling water, 8 minutes, until tender. Drain and trim away tough inner core. Chop coarsely and mix with sauce. Place in buttered 2-quart casserole. Top with bread crumbs, and dot crumbs with tiny pinches of butter.

4. Bake 20 minutes.

Makes 6–8 servings.

Vernon's Kuntry Katfish

CONROE, TEXAS

*V*ernon's One-Stop used to be the *only* place to stop along Route 105 west of the interstate. The modest convenience store, an hour from Houston, sold bait and tackle and barbecue sandwiches to people heading out to fish on Lake Conroe, and it served as a refuge where the outdoors set could linger on their way back home to commiserate with Vernon Bowers about the big bass or crappie that got away. One day, in the early 1980s, Vernon and a pal were watching the traffic go by when they had a brainstorm. Wouldn't all these anglers who were leaving empty handed, with no fish to fry, really appreciate a nice catfish supper?

The restaurant Mr. Bowers and his friend conceived, called Vernon's Kuntry Katfish, is now a destination treasured not only by the outdoors set, but by hordes of hungry Aggies from Texas A&M in nearby College Station, as well as adventurous Houstonians who drive up from the city for a true country . . . er, *kuntry* meal. (We who worry about the English language had to know immediately, before opening the menu, about the erratic spelling of the restaurant's name. Vernon's wife, Mary Bowers, explained with cheerful nonchalance, "We used Ks instead of Cs because it seemed unique. We thought that up, Daddy [her pet name for Vernon] and I.") The original ten-table café has expanded four times, and the dirt parking lot has been paved. On a good day, one-thousand meals are served, and Monday through Friday at lunchtime, there is always a wait.

"The people know a good thing when they taste it," explained U.S. Senator Phil Gramm of Texas, who, with his wife, Wendy Lee Gramm, joined us for lunch at Vernon's on a Saturday in the fall. We had asked the senator, who taught economics in College Station for twelve years before running for office, to suggest a true Lone Star State eating experience for us to write about. Vernon's Kuntry Katfish was his choice. "For the vegetables!" he rejoiced, extolling the kitchen's daily selection of such downhome delights as turnip greens, northern beans, field peas, and pickled green tomatoes. "It's hard to get good vegetables like this any more," he said, lamenting that, when he is in Washington, D.C., he starves for the fare most of his fellow Texans take for granted: barbecue, Tex-Mex, and country-style vegetables.

"And just look at this catfish," added Wendy Gramm, who also taught economics at Texas A&M before entering public service and becoming chairman of the U.S. Commodity Futures Trading Commission. Mrs. Gramm poked her fork at a thick, sandy-surfaced piece of fried fish, prodding it just hard enough to crack the filet's exterior and reveal glistening white meat, venting aromatic steam into the air. "Look how plump it is; look how it falls into nice, big flakes." Vernon's white shank filets, cut from farm-raised Mississippi fish, are tightly hugged by a flour-and-cornmeal crust with just enough seasoned zest to amplify their essential sweetness. The meat itself is so flavorful that even the menu's anomalous broiled catfish, merely seasoned but without the added luxury of the mudpuppy's traditional breading and hot-oil bath, has a voluptuous richness reminiscent of prime beef.

The appeal of Vernon's Kuntry Katfish transcends delectable food. Although it is several miles west of Conroe's business district, the easy-going restaurant has become a community gathering place, with the full flavor of an old-fashioned fish-camp dining room where neighbors congregate at big tables under spinning overhead fans to shoot the breeze or celebrate a special occasion. Here is where church groups and school clubs come for their banquets, where the senior citizens' Friendship Center holds its annual fish-fry fund raiser, and where Thanksgiving turkeys by the score are cooked and given away to local charities that serve needy citizens.

"Can I have everyone's attention, please!" calls a waitress at the height of the lunch hour in the middle of the main dining room. She puts her hand on the shoulder of a white-haired matriarch sitting at a large table with her children, grandchildren, and two babies from yet another generation of her family. "This is Gladys," the waitress calls above the din. Today is her birthday, so can you all please help me sing to her?" Throughout the restaurant, forks drop and iced tea tumblers clink down on the laminated tables, as a hundred people break out in a round of "Happy Birthday" and Gladys beams with joy. She blows out the single candle on her cupcake, offers a shy wave of thanks to the friends and strangers who have serenaded her and, within two seconds of the song's end, the room is once again filled with the clatter and conversation of happy eaters.

For us out-of-towners, one of the great joys of coming to Vernon's Kuntry Katfish, other than the food and the convivial country ambiance, is people watching. Here, every day at noon, is a bonanza of Texas individuals you won't likely meet an hour south in the cosmopolitan city of Houston: a bullnecked young man, in a swoop-brimmed black Stetson and Roper boots, who looks like a professional steer wrestler; a rickety old farm hand wearing his cleanest one-piece jumpsuit, accompanied by his wife in a flowered dress that looks straight out of the Sears catalogue, circa 1956; a table full of buoyant high-school athletes in their lavishly ornamented letter sweaters; an octogenarian college professor in a turtleneck and black beret reading a book of sonnets as he dines; a serious young backwoods couple in matching camouflage fatigues feeding catfish and jalapeño hushpuppies to their three babies, all under two years old.

The strangest thing about the crowd at Vernon's on the Saturday we ate there with Phil and Wendy Gramm was that it was about seventy-five percent women. When we puzzled aloud about this curious demographic, the senator reminded us of the favorite pastime of so many of his fellow Texans. "Today is the first Saturday in November," he grinned with pride. "It is the opening day of deer season. So, I would say that the men are hunting. You know, in the Senate, we take off the Christian holidays and the Jewish holidays. I've long thought we should take off the opening day of hunting season, too. We need to respect the needs of the temporal man."

In fact, we never did meet Vernon Bowers. We timed our visit to his restaurant so that it would coincide with the arrival of our Texas good-eats tipster, Senator Gramm, who had come to town to attend a momentous Aggie–Sooner football game in College Station. But, because deer season had just begun, Vernon was gone. Neither the epic pigskin rivalry nor the visit of a United States senator, and certainly not the presence of a couple of food writers from the East, were enough to dissuade him from his priority. The Saturday of the big game, Vernon's wife, Mary, and his son Buster told us that Daddy and his pals were already deep in the Texas countryside near the town named Hunt, with plenty of beefsteak and shrimp kabobs to tide them over, as well as all the fixin's to cook venison chili.

Good Pie

Dessert in Vernon's family-favored catfish parlor is a big deal, and it is an honest reflection of the way country people cook: an iconoclastic blend of convenience products and traditions. The banana pudding, for example, is a classic, made with vanilla wafers that soften in the custard to the consistency of moist cake. There are shockingly sweet fruit or pecan cobblers, and brownies piled high with ice cream and fudge sauce. The best and most evocative dessert is the one called good pie, *so named because, after he first made it—from a recipe supplied by a canned milk salesperson—Vernon overheard a customer exclaim, "This is* good!*" While it may not be the sort of innocent farm food about which we urban food writers sometimes fantasize, it is what wins blue ribbons at state fairs, and keeps happy customers coming back to Vernon's Kuntry Katfish.*

1 14-ounce can sweetened condensed milk (Vernon's uses Eagle Brand)

1 pound cream cheese, softened

2 8-inch baked pie shells

4–6 fresh ripe bananas, thinly sliced

1 20-ounce can crushed pineapple, drained

2 cups heavy cream, well-chilled and whipped

1 cup chopped pecans, toasted

$^1/_2$ cup chocolate syrup

1. Use an electric mixer to blend the condensed milk and cream cheese to a smooth consistency. Spread the mixture in the pie shells and freeze until firm (a minimum of 2 hours, but they may be made to this point and frozen in advance).

2. About an hour before serving, add layers of the sliced bananas and pineapple. Spread whipped cream over the top. Sprinkle whipped cream with chopped pecans and drizzle with chocolate syrup. Refrigerate for 1 hour before serving.

Makes 2 8-inch pies.

Woolworth's Lunch Counter

SANTA FE, NEW MEXICO

*B*efore it went out of business and reopened as a Foot Locker shoe store in 1998, Woolworth's on the plaza in Santa Fe was a great place to eat. As in so many distinguished restaurants, it wasn't only the food that made a meal at the dime-store lunch counter so special, but the ambiance, the service, the *je ne sais quois* of the whole dining experience.

The magic included that distinct Woolworth's aroma that combines dry goods, lamp shades, liniments, face creams, and penny candy, with a long lunch counter and an open grill. It was the kind of five-and-ten that had everything: pain relievers and underwear, small appliances and a jumbo gumball machine. In the market for perfume? Here they had a shelf of Elite Parfum—from Paris, the label said—on sale at $3.97 for 3.3 ounces; scents included Odeon, Pandora, Ice Gem, and a bright purple one called Fire. Some of the inventory was distinctly New Mexican: sacks of blue popcorn, inexpensive copper-colored concho belts, silly Indian archery sets with suction-cup arrows, and prints of magnificent historical photographs taken by B. G. Randall at the Taos Pueblo in 1905. Even toward the end of its tenure, as Santa Fe became a paradigm of New West style, this Woolworth's had small-city charm that transcended fashion.

The lunch counter ran nearly the whole length of the store, its orange-upholstered stools matched by Naugahyde booths for table dining. Its menu featured roast tom turkey with dressing and cranberry sauce, liver and onions, and baked meatloaf with gravy—all served on unbreakable plates under bright fluorescent lights. Woolworth's also offered local specialties, but not of the swanky, bright-young-chef variety. There were chili cheeseburgers, tortillaburgers, chili dogs, burritos, and bowls of red or green chili with Saltines. The pièce de resistance, at the counter seats as well as at the take-out stand up front, was Fritos pie. In the mid-1990s, a giant Fritos pie cost four dollars. It was a big trough of crisp corn chips blanketed with meat-and-bean red or green chili and a heap of shredded orange cheese. Chopped onions and sliced jalapeño peppers were optional.

Fritos pie is an inspired combination of ingredients. Unlike almost any other food except, perhaps, a hot-fudge sundae in which the ice cream melts as it warms and the fudge clots as it cools, it dramatically changes consistency while you eat it. The dynam-ics of a Fritos pie are not thermal, how-ever, they are more a matter of textural flux. The Fritos start crisp but, as soon as the chili is ladeled on, they begin to soften. Those chips completely inun-dated at the bottom of the trough thicken, gradually becoming an earthy cornmeal pad underneath the spicy meat and beans. Other chips at the edge of the trough and, therefore, unblanketed by chili, or those at the very bottom, where they are protected by moistened chips above them, retain varying degrees of crispness, providing crunch to balance the pie's tender parts. And, because the chili is dolloped onto the chips hot from its kettle, the shreds of cheese that go

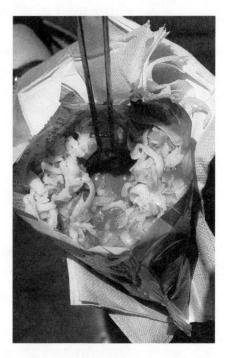

atop it liquefy instantly. Only the bottommost shreds melt, blending into the meaty brew and becoming veins of butterfatty goodness. The cheese at the very top stays dry and retains its crumbly texture.

In the early days of the Fritos pie, it was sold to go, served directly inside a Fritos bag. Each pie was made simply by ripping open a wax-paper bag of Fritos (small or large) and piling in all the other ingre-dients, then planting a plastic fork in the center. The bag was a perfect container, easy to gobble from on a park bench or while on a stroll.

The person who configured the Frito pie in its now-classic arrange-ment worked at Woolworth's until the day it closed. Teresa Hernandez came to Santa Fe from the nearby mining town of Madrid in the early

1950s. She was impressed by a dish served at local drive-ins: a paper-cupful of chili on a bed of shredded lettuce, garnished with a handful of Frito chips. She recalled, "When I came to work at Woolworth's, I thought maybe we could make a different kind of Frito pie. My idea was to elim-inate the lettuce and to use the Fritos on the bottom. Mr. Donald Skelton, who was the manager then, and myself, we decided to use a Frito bag instead of the paper cup. Schoolchildren liked it the most. They used to come in after school or during their lunch hour and buy Frito pies so they could eat them while they walked around the plaza. That's what's good about a Frito pie: You can eat it sitting down or on your way to work. It's so easy."

However, lunch-counter manager Liz Talamante explained, the Frito company changed the bag's consistency. "The new bags weren't strong enough," she says. "The chili leaked. No one wants a wet-bottomed Frito pie." Styrofoam bowls and cardboard boats (for regular and jumbo, respec-tively) were substituted and, while the ingredients were as good as ever, the presentation suffered.

Cliff Mills, the store manager (and grandson of photographer B. G. Randall), explained, "Everybody who is anybody in Santa Fe eats at Wool-worth's"; to prove his point, he enumerated many state-government offi-cials who have dined on Frito pie as well as such visiting connoisseurs as Carol Burnett, Paula Abdul, Terry Bradshaw, Donald Sutherland, and "Mean" Joe Green. Celebrity clientele notwithstanding, it was always the loyalty of ordinary townsfolk that made Woolworth's Frito pie a culinary star. We witnessed one man in mechanic's overalls step up to the crowded takeout counter around lunchtime on a crisp October day and announce to one and all that it was his birthday. "A giant Frito pie!" he expansively decreed to Ms. Talamante behind the counter. She told him that giant pies were available only to those who were seated, and that he would have to order the next size down, a jumbo. The jubilant gentleman reconsidered a moment, then decided to shoot the works: "Two jumbos and a corn dog!" he proclaimed. He paid with a personal check for $9.11, then walked out into the Plaza, balancing two Frito pies and a dog-on-a-stick in his arms, as he looked for a park bench in the autumn air where he could kick back and relish his birthday banquet.

Fritos Pie

Mary Encinias, chili chef at Woolworth's (and former chef at the state police academy), made three five-gallon pans of red chili and one five-gallon pan of green each morning. Hers was not a sophisticated chili; the recipe is quick and simple lunch-counter fare—the only appropriate kind for Fritos pie.

RED CHILI

2 slices bacon, cut into one-inch pieces

1 clove garlic, minced

1 medium onion, chopped

1 pound ground chuck

1 teaspoon salt

2 tablespoons red chili powder

$1/2$ teaspoon ground cumin

$1/3$ cup tomato paste

$1 1/2$ cups water (approximately)

1 cup cooked pinto beans

Sauté bacon until fat is rendered. Add garlic and onion to pan and cook until onion softens. Add beef and cook until hamburger is browned, breaking up lumps with a fork. (If desired, excess fat may be poured off at this point.) Add salt, chili powder, and cumin, then tomato paste and enough water to give the chili a loose, but not soupy, consistency. Cook, 15 minutes. Stir in beans and simmer until beans are warmed through.

TO ASSEMBLE FRITOS PIES

4–5 cups Fritos chips (the better part of an 11-ounce bag)

Red chili (recipe precedes)

2 cups shredded orange cheese (Monterrey Jack preferred)

chopped onion, optional

diced jalapeño peppers, optional

To make four individual servings, use four wide, shallow bowls. In each, arrange a broad bed of Fritos chips. Ladle chili atop the chips, then sprinkle cheese atop chili. Garnish with chopped onions and jalapeño peppers, if desired.

Makes 4 jumbo Fritos pies.

Index